AF504809

B–52 Down!
The Night the Bombs Fell From the Sky

A story of impossible odds

By Linda Harris Sittig

Linda Harris Sittig

B-52 Down! The Night the Bombs Fell from the Sky

by Linda Harris Sittig

Copyright © 2024 by Linda Harris Sittig

Cover photography courtesy of the individual entities and photographers listed within this book.

The appearance of U.S. Department of Defense (DoD) visual information does not imply or constitute DoD endorsement.

All Rights Reserved.

No part of this publication may be reproduced, stored in a retrieval system or transmitted in any form or by any means, electronic, mechanical, photocopied, recorded, or otherwise, without the express written consent of the publisher.

More Praise for *B-52 Down!*

"If you have an appreciation for thorough research, you need to read this book. As a former B-52 crew member, the author's description re-kindled my emotions when carrying nuclear weapons on Chrome Dome missions. Her realistic descriptions of the final moments of flight and the use of survival kit contents transport you to being a crew member. She also captured the essence of the willingness of the local population to endure horrible weather conditions to aid in rescue efforts. A terrific read!"

Roger H. Williams, Major, United States Air Force, Ret'd

"B-52 Down! It is a riveting reconstructed account of Buzz One Four, the B-52 bomber that carried two thermonuclear bombs and crashed into a rural Maryland community during the Cold War. Linda Sittig not only captures the historical role aviation played in our national defense but gives us a true sense of the men who flew this aircraft, their families, and the ordinary citizens determined to find the missing airmen in the aftermath of this tragedy."

Captain Laura Savino, Pilot United Airlines, Retired

"Thoroughly researched by Linda Sittig, this book brought back many memories of the B-52 crash of 1964. It was fascinating to read about the families of the fliers. I thank the author for writing this book, a story that needed to be told."

Gerry Beachy, Curator, Grantsville Community Museum

This book is dedicated first and foremost to

Bucky Schriver

Without Bucky's passion for preserving local history and his unwavering belief in honoring the legacy of five men who rode the ill-fated B-52 bomber, this book would never have happened.

I also respectfully dedicate this story to Buzz One Four's crew, who risked everything in service to our country; and their families, whose lives were changed forever.

To the residents of Garrett County, and western Allegany County, Maryland, who put their lives on hold trying to rescue the five Air Force fliers, America salutes your compassion.

"I thought this would be the story of my uncle (Robert Townley). But it's not just about him or his crew. The real story is the community – the people who opened their hearts and their homes to save the lives of five men."

-Gina Townley Swinburn

When brainstorming concepts for the cover, I realized that there was no single picture that could truly capture the nature of the events that unfolded. Just as the story became about a town rather than a single person, the cover is a quilt of photographs of the people and places involved in the crash and its aftermath, reinforcing the idea of community captured within the following pages.

Table of Contents

High Flight

"Oh, I have slipped the surly bonds of earth,
And danced the skies on laughter-silvered wings;
Sunward I've climbed and joined the tumbling mirth of sun-split clouds -
and done a hundred things you have not dreamed of -
wheeled and soared and swung high in the sunlit silence.
Hovering there I've chased the shouting wind along
and flung my eager craft through footless halls of air.

"Up, up the long delirious burning blue
I've topped the wind-swept heights with easy grace,
where never lark, or even eagle, flew;
and, while with silent, lifting mind I've trod
the high untrespassed sanctity of space,
put out my hand and touched the face of God."

By Canadian fighter pilot John Gillespie Magee, Jr., 1941

Introduction

I was autographing copies of my novel, *Last Curtain Call*, in the spring of 2017 at Main Street Books in Frostburg, Maryland. A gentleman approached, introduced himself as Bucky Schriver, and said, "I have a story that would make a great book, and you'd be the perfect person to write it."

I demurely thanked him for the compliment. He did not hesitate but launched into telling me about the crash of a B-52 bomber in the mountains west of Frostburg in 1964. "It was an Air Force bomber, with a five-man crew, and two nuclear bombs on board," he declared.

His enthusiasm was admirable, but I replied that I did not write military stories about men. My specialty, I informed him, was to write about Strong Women.

He never missed a beat and said, "Well, the five men all had wives, and it's the human-interest part of the story that deserves to be told."

Again, I hesitated, telling him I had already committed to the third novel in my "Threads of Courage Series," and I wouldn't be able to tackle another story right now. Undeterred, Mr. Schriver smiled and said, "Can we exchange emails?"

Not seeing any harm, I agreed. Every three or four months, I would get an email asking me how my third book was coming and when could I consider the B-52 story?

My third novel, *Counting Crows*, was published in the fall of 2019, and by April 2020, I started hearing from Bucky on a regular basis. By then, I had to agree that his story was compelling and would make an interesting topic to research. The story would retell the actual events, but I would include the emotional aspect of the story.

In June 2020, Bucky emailed me that a niece of one of the crew, Gina Townley Swinburn, and her sister, Lisa Townley Gilbeaux, were traveling from Louisiana to Garrett County to revisit the site of the crash. Would I be interested in meeting them?

On a hot July afternoon in the lobby of a nearby travel hotel, we met, smiling through Covid-19 face-masks. That poignant encounter lasted three solid hours and made me realize how much the families had been affected by the crash.

My husband and I drove home, and I started my first draft that evening. I think I also felt the pull to honor the USAF men because my father, Bill Harris, had been a bombardier on a B-26 on D-Day, 1944.

By the time I finished the manuscript, I had interviewed over 34 people and read hundreds of pages of research material. I learned more about nuclear bombs, how to eject from an incapacitated plane at 30,000 feet, and weather conditions in blinding blizzards, than I ever could have imagined.

But more importantly, I was given the opportunity to write about the crew's families, the people of the western Maryland mountains who formed the remarkable rescue teams, and the five-man crew themselves, who valiantly gave all they had.

This, then, is *B-52 Down! The Night the Bombs Fell from The Sky.*

22 YEARS BEFORE OUR STORY STARTS
November 21, 1943

The following is an account of a B-17 Bomber that crashed in 1943 in the mountains of western Maryland. What makes this article so eerie is that the almost same scenario happened again in 1964, but with a different outcome.

The B-17 pilot, strapped in and adjusting his harness, gave himself an imaginary thumbs up. *Another routine flight, hope nothing's out of the ordinary.*

His plane had earned the nickname Flying Fortress for a reason. Ask anyone in the Army Air Corps, and they'd nod their head. The B-17 Bomber did its job protecting freedom during World War II. Boeing designed the B-17 in the 1930s as a stellar bomber, and pilots preferred B-17s due to their excellent stability and superior electrical systems.

The pilot loved the small compact body of a B-17, but still, a deep breath escaped his lungs. Even seasoned pilots like himself knew that something could always go wrong, even on routine flights. Ultimately, he only needed to keep his plane on a steady course for Pittsburgh. He checked. Yes, the other four US Army Transport crew members had strapped in and were ready for takeoff.

The last steps entailed tightening his helmet straps, rechecking his north-east course, and engaging the engines. As the aircraft gained momentum down the runway, he pushed up on the throttle and nosed the plane into the air.

There was something magical about being airborne, and the sensation always sent a jolt of exhilaration through his veins. Snug in a winter fleece-lined flight suit like the rest of his crew, he said a silent prayer for safety.

But not long after takeoff, the plane flew into heavy fog, and the number four engine conked out.

Okay, one engine down, but the other three seem okay. Poor visibility, though.

Sometime later, he noticed ice forming on the wings, a significant problem. And his fuel gauge now showed dangerously low levels. The best choice was to bail out.

He pushed the eject signal. BAIL OUT! BAIL OUT! BAIL OUT! Then he waited for the three enlisted men to discharge first. Next, he set the plane on auto-pilot, and he and the copilot bailed. At an altitude of about 7,000 feet, the five-man crew dropped through the air and landed near Ebensburg, Pennsylvania, roughly 26 miles west of Altoona.

The B-17 stormed solo for an additional 80 miles south before skimming Savage Mountain below Frostburg, Maryland, and then crashing into a rugged hillside when it ran out of fuel.

But Lady Luck accompanied the men. The pilot and copilot landed in a wooded area, and the other three crew members set down in a large open field near each other. The Pennsylvania State Police retrieved the five men before the sunset.

Cold but grateful to be alive.

In 1964, precisely 22 years, one month, and 24 days later, another Air Force Bomber, this time a B-52, entered those same winter skies. The B-52 plane also carried a five-man crew on a Sunday night, but hit a blinding snowstorm and violent turbulence.

The massiveness of a B-52, literally half the length of a football field, made this plane the king of the skies. A stealth bomber that was the prize of the U.S. Air Force, equipped to lead the fight in the Cold War against the Soviet Union, but not perhaps against a mammoth blizzard.

And this particular B-52, called Buzz One Four, was carrying two thermonuclear bombs.

Day One

January 12, 1964

Major Thomas W. McCormick – Pilot of Buzz One Four, age 44, from Yawkey, West Virginia. Photo courtesy of BuzzOneFour.org.

Sunday, January 12, 1964
Daytime temperature, Turner Air Force Base, Albany, Georgia: 55°

Major Robert Payne awakened to the security phone ringing in his house early Sunday morning. He answered and listened to the message that he had to assemble a crew to go to Westover Air Base in Chicopee, Massachusetts. They were to retrieve a B-52 Bomber.

Fay Payne recognized the familiar ring and surmised her husband had an important call from the base.

"Gotta go back in." Bob nodded to her. "I have to assemble a crew for a retrieval mission."

"On a Sunday?"

"Yep." He showered, shaved, and dressed, then headed to his office.

Once there, he selected the crew of Pilot Tom McCormick. Unfortunately, the regular navigator was on alert duty and could not go on this mission. Shrugging, Payne penciled in his name on the roster. He'd take the other guy's place.

Then he returned home.

"Why you? You're supposed to be off-duty today."

"The regular navigator isn't available, and they need a full five-man crew to fly up to Massachusetts. I'll fill in as navigator."

"When do you have to leave?"

"I need to get back to the office, so, within the hour." Bob went to the bedroom closet and retrieved an overnight fly bag.

At age forty-two, Fay mused, she shouldn't feel annoyed when family plans had to change. This Sunday wasn't the first time. Oh well, she'd bake a cherry pie and save some for Bob when he returned tomorrow. It would make him grin.

Had it been over twenty years since they first met and then married in Tulsa, Oklahoma? She smiled; he was as handsome today at 6 feet tall with his ruddy complexion and warm brown eyes as the day they first met.

Bob came to the kitchen and kissed her.

She followed him to the door as he hustled down the front walk.

"Bob, wait! Did you pack a warm flight jacket? It's probably colder in Massachusetts."

"No time to hunt for one. It's just overnight; I'll see you tomorrow." Then he waved and walked off.

Fay looked up at the crisp blue Georgia sky and crossed her fingers. Please let them have good weather. Then she fixed lunch for their three kids, Bill, Robert, and her young daughter, Teresa.

Before Bob turned the corner, he patted his pocket to ensure that he had brought along his lucky silver dollar.

Dorismarie McCormick had been married to her Air Force husband, Tom McCormick, for almost twenty years. But saying good-bye as he walked out the door for a mission still caused her an unconscious frown and purposeful silent prayers.

Tom's flight crew, all off-duty, had been called back. At least this assignment didn't have the danger like their Chrome Dome flights. This time the men would just be on a short trip to Massachusetts to bring a B-52 back to Georgia. She had hoped she and Tom would be having a peaceful Sunday afternoon, but military plans often changed that.

A semi-mild Georgia day graced Turner Air Force Base. The 55 degrees pulled her back to childhood winters in southern California. And if she inhaled deeply, she could almost detect the sweet memory-smell of her grandfather's orange groves with their spicy scent of citrus.

A moderate winter day at Turner wasn't exactly California, but still a gift.

At thirty-nine, Dorismarie had managed to keep her figure, even after having two babies. Standing at six feet, she came close to matching her husband in height—the tallest among the military wives.

Everyone enjoyed Dorismarie's extroverted, friendly personality. She collected friends quickly with her broad smile and good sense of humor. Stylish with hair the color of espresso coffee, she had once dreamed of being a graphic artist. Instead, she had become an Air Force wife.

Turner Air Force Base hosted the perfect spot for a training field.

Only four miles from downtown Albany, Georgia, the location provided temperate weather plus a semi-flat terrain. Dorismarie and Tom usually moved every two years with the Air Force, and it always took time to re-adjust. They were now enjoying their more extended tour at Turner, where Tom's unit, the 484th Bombardment Wing, had been activated.

Being a seasoned military spouse, Dorismarie didn't waste time brooding about the schedule. She looked around after Tom left for the air-field and spied the last Christmas decorations. She should put them away. But with Michael off at college and Tommy at a neighbor's, she could use the time to continue working on her newest painting.

As the radio began a Patsy Cline tune, she walked over and picked up her brushes. Later, she'd start supper. Perhaps she'd make some enchiladas for Tommy with the leftover chicken from last night. Cooking Mexican food brought back the taste of southern California and always made her hungry.

For Command Pilot, Major Thomas W. McCormick, today's task would be a quick recovery mission. His five-man crew would only fly from Turner to Westover Air Force Base in Chicopee, Massachusetts.

The bomber they were to retrieve had been flying a Chrome Dome flight when engine failure had forced the pilot to land in Spain. Mechanics performed preliminary repairs, and then the aircraft needed to return to its Georgia base for final repairs. However, due to weather problems, this plane, Buzz One Four, terminated the run at Westover. The Air Force needed a new crew since the original team of exhausted men had run out of duty time.

Tom took this job as seriously as any other. Even when tinkering out in the garage, he researched every project with the thoroughness and self-discipline that permeated his military life.

The Chrome Dome missions were a strategic operation of the Cold War from 1958 to 1968.

Starting shortly after World War II's conclusion in 1945, the Cold War emerged as a geopolitical tension-filled era. The United States and the Soviet Union engaged in a stand-off that focused on both superpowers having the potential to utilize nuclear bombs.

Since America dropped two atomic bombs on Japan in August of 1945, nuclear warfare between countries had become a real possibility. Although the Soviet Union and the United States had been allies during World War II with the combined effort of defeating Adolf Hitler, their allegiances changed after 1947.

Operation Chrome Dome, instituted by Strategic Air Command (SAC), became a combat-ready defense strategy. Twelve B-52 Bombers patrolled three air routes on continuous twenty-four-hour missions. Each strategic heavy bomber armed with thermonuclear weapons flew to points located on the fringe of Soviet airspace.

The theory stood that if the Soviet Union initiated nuclear aggression against America, the Chrome Dome B-52s would be within striking distance to retaliate and attack the Soviet Union.

The men who became Chrome Dome pilots had trained at air bases in California before being assigned to other locations. All the airmen at Turner were a select essential part of preventing the spread of communism.

The motto of the SAC became, "Peace is Our Profession." And the crew of Buzz One Four took that to heart.

Buzz One Four and the other Chrome Dome bombers supported The Cold War, which lasted from 1947 until December 1991, when the Soviet Union dissolved into 15 sovereign post-soviet states.

As Tom rode to the airfield, two boys pedaled past on their Sears Roebuck bikes. Usually a serious-minded but good-humored guy, the unexpected bicycle scene erased the smile off his face. How long had it taken for him to get a bike growing up in West Virginia coal country southwest of Charleston?

Money had always been an issue, just like with other coal-mining families, where dinner sometimes might only be a plate of beans with biscuits. And although Tom had considered college, perhaps even becoming an engineer, the fastest way to escape the Appalachian coalfields was to join the military.

He wanted to become a fighter pilot, but his 6-foot 4-inch height disqualified him. His large frame would not fit inside a tight fighter cockpit. Instead, he could become a combat military pilot. In June 1941, one month before his 20th birthday and six months shy of the Japanese attack on Pearl Harbor, he had enlisted. Within two years, Tom became commissioned as an officer within the Army Air Corps. After additional training, he became an Army Air Corps pilot, flying in World War II[1].

God, had the war been twenty years ago?

While he had escaped the coalfields, he couldn't fight the descending sadness as he remembered that so many fellow service men did not make it home from the war.

---

1 - The US Air Force did not form until 1947.

But he managed to do so. His good fortune continued as he met Dorismarie Healy at a dance in California. They married in February 1944. When World War II officially ended on September 2, 1945, he returned stateside.

Now, driving toward his current mission with the bikers in his rear view mirror, he shook his head to clear the memories and concentrate instead on today's assignment. As the crew pilot, Tom always felt a keen sense of responsibility for the other four men, and he wouldn't allow memories kindled by boys on bikes to jeopardize that.

On the other side of the base, on North Carolina Avenue, where many of the enlisted airmen lived with their families in duplex homes, quiet 27-year-old Melvin Wooten kissed his wife, Carol, and reassured her he'd be back tomorrow.

Carol Wooten's smile thinned. She did not want Mel to leave.

Unlike some other husbands, Melvin helped out with the kids, seven-year-old Jerry Jay, 18-month-old Deanna, and now a newborn daughter, Debbie. Carol had given birth 11 days ago and would love to have Melvin off-duty just a bit longer.

She remembered when their son was born a preemie and needed to stay a month longer in the hospital. Melvin had hocked his private pistol so they could pay the hospital fees. He was like that, she mused, putting her and the kids first.

The youngest of Tom McCormick's crew and their gunner, Melvin had an easy-going personality with a boyish countenance and sandy brown hair. At first glance, one would think he might still be a high school or even college athlete, but he had enlisted at 18 and ascended to the coveted rank of technical sergeant. Now he was only two levels away from the top enlisted rank, having traded his childhood in Texas for the Air Force's open skies.

As Melvin approached the airfield, a nervous tinge of excitement erupted. He often wondered if the other guys got that same feeling before every flight. He might not have as many years' experience as the rest of the crew, but he had the enthusiasm and work ethic to be a good team player.

Hoping his wife would cope with the three kids alone, he carried his flight bag and walked off whistling.

In the duplex, Carol put the baby in the bassinette and went to the kitchen looking for some quick Chef Boy-Ar-Dee she could fix for lunch. Now at twenty-three, caring for two young children and a newborn, opening a can of pasta was about all she had the energy for.

As Melvin left, she could feel a headache starting.

Robert Townley, the third Air Force Major on the crew, retrieved his flight bag.

His wife, Gene (Imogene), respected her husband's unwavering commitment to his job. He tackled every assignment with steadfast dedication and enthusiasm, and she admired that about him. They were both from Gadsden, Alabama, about an hour's drive northeast from Birmingham. To Gene, family was the most crucial aspect of her life.

Gene, more than the other military wives, didn't let the schedule changes get to her. She busied herself, taking care of their six-year-old son Reed and writing to their older son, Don.

Frugal, recycling even before that became in vogue, Gene loved a good sale, even when she could have afforded to buy the merchandise at full price. And with a sense of taking care of others, she became renowned for her famous peanut butter milkshakes, sure to bring a smile to any guest.

So, when Robert went on a mission, she worked on projects until he returned.

As Robert left the house and headed for the airfield, he took in a deep breath. The hint of spring entered his mind.

Only two months till baseball season.

He'd been a high school coach and now used those talents to head up the Little League at Turner. Even at 4,900 acres, Turner had that small-town community feel. And for an extrovert like Robert, that was fine.

Tall at just under six feet, with dark brown eyes to match his hair, he had grown up in Gadsden, Alabama. His family had lived in a narrow, deep house out on Albany Avenue. The structure only accommodated two bedrooms and no inside plumbing. Hard to remember how he and his other three siblings had managed in a two-bedroom house, but it had been home, and his memories were happy ones.

Shaking his head to clear the cobwebs of the past, he brought his attention to today's assignment and his job as the radar navigator. This position always meant being confined to the infamous Black Hole below deck, but tight spaces never bothered him.

Captain Parker Peedin, nicknamed Mack, was the copilot. Outgoing, movie-star handsome, and a snappy dresser, his gregarious personality attracted people to him like flies to honey. He'd grown up in Smithfield, North Carolina, 30 miles southeast of Raleigh. But unlike the senior members of the crew, Mack did not join the military during World War II.

Born in 1934, he had been ten years old when Majors McCormick, Payne, and Townley were already flying. He and Melvin Wooten were the younger members of the crew at 29 and 27 years of age.

Even as a teenager, Mack showed a self-assured industriousness: a Boy Scout who dabbled in photography later landing a position on his high school newspaper and yearbook staff. President of his senior class and a star athlete, he had lettered in football and basketball at Selma High School.

Mack was jaunty and a prankster. His cousin, Joyce Bowman, years later would remark that thinking of Mack reminded her of Hawkeye Pierce, the sharp-witted doctor with a proverbial sense of humor on the television series, M*A*S*H.

Perhaps the most telling text about Mack's early years is the quote in his 1953 high school yearbook – "Best All-Around" (male). Interestingly, Dianne Britton, the senior girl dubbed "Best All-Around," is whom Mack married in 1955 when they were both twenty years old.

Even at a young age, Mack held a fascination with airplanes. While enrolled at North Carolina State in Raleigh, he took flying lessons and loved to swoop low over his mother's house in nearby Selma. By February 1963, he had become a US Air Force Pilot stationed at Turner.

On this particular Sunday, Mack received the same call as the rest of the crew – he had to go back on duty to retrieve a B-52 bomber from Massachusetts.

Dianne just sighed. When those calls came, the men had no choice. You dropped whatever you were doing and suited up.

Mack had been the focus of her life ever since high school. Dianne, an attractive brunette, could most likely have had her pick of any of the boys at Selma High. But she chose Mack Peedin. Life with him would be exciting.

She attended East Carolina University for two years and then left to marry Mack. Never once did she anticipate the worry that came with being an Air Force pilot's wife. Unlike other wives who contented themselves with purchases on the base, Dianne often drove herself into town where the newer fashions advertised in Ladies Home Journal were available. She never lost her sense of style.

Dianne kissed Mack but then grabbed his arm. "You be careful, you hear?"

"Sweetheart, I'm always careful," he grinned.

Captain Parker 'Mack' Peedin – Copilot of Buzz One Four, age 29, from Smithfield, North Carolina. Photo courtesy of BuzzOneFour.org.

Day Two

January 13, 1964

Major Robert L. Payne – Navigator of Buzz One Four, age 41, from Tulsa, Oklahoma. Photo courtesy of BuzzOneFour.org.

Monday, January 13, 1964
Westover AFB, Chicopee, Massachusetts: 22° F
Philipsburg, Pennsylvania: 14° F

On February 1, 1963, airmen of the new 484th Bombardment Wing stationed at Turner Air Force Base, Albany, Georgia, were now part of the Chrome Dome Operation. They would fly three 24-hour missions per month on alert for Soviet aggression toward the United States.

All five men, Thomas McCormick, Parker Peedin, Robert Townley, Robert Payne and Melvin Wooten were part of that 484th Bombardment Wing assigned to work together as a B–52 crew. But they were more than just an air unit; they were colleagues.

The small group joked with each other as they climbed the transport flight to Massachusetts and arrived at dusk. Once at Westover Air Force Base, the crew greeted the exhausted men who had just flown in at 3 p.m. from Soviet air space with their B-52, Buzz One Four.

A short briefing had occurred back at Turner. Command Pilot Tom McCormick received an additional briefing at Westover to include rechecking the proposed flight path to Georgia, the expected weather, and emergency procedures.

"Okay, men. We're used to these B-52s. Only difference this time is we'll be carrying two nuclear bombs."

Mack Peedin grinned while Melvin Wooten's eyebrows shot up in surprise. They'd never carried bombs like this before.

There was no discussion about the possibility of foul weather.

They ate dinner together and went to the accommodations area to grab a few hours rest before takeoff time at 12:38 a.m.

"Damn, it's cold," grumbled Bob Payne. At 22 degrees outside, he fervently wished he had brought a proper winter flight jacket.

"Come on, Bob, you'll be home by breakfast. Just think about one of your wife's cherry pies." Robert Townley thumped Payne on the back.

Bob Payne lay down on a cot and threw an extra blanket over himself. "Still can't wait to get back to Georgia."

Thirty minutes before takeoff, the crew zipped up their flight suits, boarded Buzz One Four, and began their pre-flight check.

Major McCormick and Captain Mack Peedin climbed into the cockpit and checked the controls.

After discovering a small oxygen leak back in the tail gunner's position, Tech Sergeant Melvin Wooten moved up to the upper flight deck. Once there, he lowered himself into the electronic warfare officer's seat.

Major Townley and Major Payne climbed down below deck to the Black Hole. As Townley, the bombardier, eased himself into the small windowless area, Payne sat next to him.

Although they joked how they were all looking forward to some good old Georgia sunshine, each crew member took the job seriously.

The flight back would only take two hours and thirty-seven minutes.

Major McCormick checked his oxygen mask and nodded to Captain Peedin. Using the intercom, he asked for a crew check from each man. He ended with his no-nonsense reminder, "pins out, ready for takeoff." This command ensured that the men checked the ejection mechanisms for operational mode.

Before the actual take-off, each man said a private prayer for safety and then congratulated himself for having one of the best jobs in the US Air Force, a B-52 Bomber crew member. Looking around, each man marveled once again at the powerful magnitude of the aircraft he flew.

Then Major McCormick taxied the plane down the runway. At the precise predetermined moment, he and Copilot Peedin pushed up the eight throttles, engaging the eight Pratt and Whitney engines to lift the B-52 skyward.

And then they were climbing, climbing, climbing, heading for 31,000 feet.

Designed to be a nuclear sentinel, the Stratofortress B-52 Bomber was a hulking monstrosity that resembled a prehistoric flying reptile. Boeing debuted the plane in 1952.

The aircraft measured 156 feet long, almost equal to a football field's width, sideline to sideline. The massive drooping swept-back wings together spanned 185 feet, half a football field's length—goal post to the 50-yard line. Three sturdy bolts connect the 48-feet high tail, the equivalent of four stories. Once fully loaded, the plane weighed 450,000 pounds, the equivalent of 30 African male elephants.

These aeronautical machines had a range of 8,000 miles before having to refuel inflight. Their payload included the capacity to carry a nuclear bomb measuring 8 feet in diameter and 25 feet in length. Altogether, the planes could carry up to 60,000 pounds of conventional bombs. Eight turbojets under the wings carried the B-52 aloft at a max speed of 638 miles per hour.

Technically known as a Stratofortress, the B-52s were heavy bombers within the Chrome Dome Operation's aerial routes. A force to be reckoned with, a B-52 could deploy its bombs from eight miles high, out of the range of antiaircraft guns.

They were the backbone of the US Air Force throughout the Cold War years, and in 1957, the production of Buzz One Four cost $6.9 million[1].

---

1 - The cost in 2020 would be 65.5 million dollars.

File photo courtesy of NOAA shows a spiraling blizzard, similar to the intensity of the storm on January 12 that the crew of Buzz One Four encountered.

Monday, January 13, 1964
Early morning temperature, Grantsville, Maryland: 12° F

Major McCormick noted with satisfaction that they had taken off on time at 12:38 a.m. Staring straight ahead, he marveled at the beauty of the universe. You couldn't help but feel closer to God when soaring into the heavens, and hopefully, they would outpace any potential storms.

Captain Peedin loved the freedom that flying brought. Once in flight, he escaped the humdrum schedule he led back on earth. Flying gave him a reprieve from having to impress anyone other than himself.

Major Townley approached every flight with commitment. He had fought in World War II, then after the war, taught high school. When the Korean War reared, Townley re-enlisted. After that, he made the military his full-time career. The motto of the Strategic Air Command, "Peace is our Profession," embedded itself in his soul.

For Major Payne, the Air Force reinforced his sense of duty to his country. He had entered the military as an aviation cadet in his home state of Oklahoma in November 1942.

Twenty-two years later, he became a Major in the US Air Force.

Tech Sergeant Wooten grew up learning to be self-reliant at an early age. Perhaps this innate sense of self-preservation led him to join the military right out of high school.

Fifty minutes into the fight, as the crew headed south, passing by Phillipsburg, Pennsylvania, the plane encountered instability in the weather.

The entire crew had experienced turbulence before, but this havoc progressed at an alarming rate. They had left Massachusetts early with the hope of avoiding any bad weather. The plane had flown directly into an unexpected violent winter storm, later called the blizzard of the century.

Sweeping in from the west, a swath of warm, unstable air slammed into a wall of frigid arctic air racing down from the north. Simultaneously, the Jetstream with winds of up to 167 miles per hour tore up from the southwest.

When all three forces collided, the fierce blizzard with colossal wind shears ruptured the night sky. At the storm's central collision point, Buzz One Four raced at 500 miles per hour.

As the tempest slammed the aircraft, Major McCormick reacted by instinct, knowing the plane could not withstand the sheer power of gale-force winds and a blizzard bombarding it on all sides. He had already radioed to Cleveland Air Traffic Center just minutes before, alerting the tower of Buzz One Four's predicament.

Now, just minutes into the storm, McCormick radioed back to Cleveland.

0634 GMT [1]
Buzz One Four: *Cleveland Center, Buzz One Four, over.*
Cleveland: *Buzz One Four, Cleveland, go-ahead.*
Buzz One Four: *Ah, roger, we're experiencing more turbulence at present.*
Cleveland: *Roger, would you like a change in altitude?*
Buzz One Four: *Ah, roger, we'd like to descend to flight level, ah, two nine zero* [2]. *Over.*
Cleveland: *Buzz One Four, roger, stand by.*

0635 GMT *(1:35 a.m.)*
Cleveland: *Ah, Buzz One Four, Cleveland, can you do a higher altitude?*
Buzz One Four: *If you can't clear us down to twenty-nine* [3], *ah, we'll climb up to three-three* [4].
Cleveland: *Buzz One Four, Cleveland, descend and maintain flight level two*

---

1 - This is Greenwich Mean Time or Coordinated Universal Time and would be the equivalent of 1:35 a.m. Eastern Standard Time, local time for the crew.
2 - 29,000 feet
3 - 29,000 feet
4 - 33,000 feet

nine zero, and if, ah, if that's not any good, you can give us a call, and we'll climb you back up.
Buzz One Four: *Roger, descending to flight level two nine zero.*

0637 GMT *(1:37 a.m.)*
Buzz One Four: *Cleveland, this is, ah, Buzz One Four, we're experiencing--- we've just left three one zero (31,000), we're passing three zero (30,000), and we're still in it.*
Cleveland: *Buzz One Four, would you say your remarks again? I was talking to Washington on another line.*
Buzz One Four: *Ah, Cleveland, Buzz One Four, we're climbing back up to three-three zero (33,000 feet).*
Cleveland: *Buzz One Four, roger, stand by one.*

McCormick and Peedin wrestled with the controls, trying desperately to keep the vast wings level as the storm battered the aircraft.

0638 GMT *(1:38 a.m.)*
Cleveland: *Buzz One Four, climb and maintain flight level three-three zero.*
Buzz One Four: unintelligible garble
Cleveland: *Buzz One Four, did you copy?*
Buzz One Four: more unintelligible sounds
Cleveland: *Ah, Buzz One Four, you're barely readable now, climb and maintain flight level three-three zero.*

0639 GMT *(1:39 a.m.)*
Cleveland: *Ah, Buzz One Four?*
The only sound from Buzz One Four was the sound of radio static.

0643 GMT *(1:43 a.m.)*
Cleveland: *Washington, do you have any contact with Buzz One Four?*
Washington: *Not yet, Cleveland. Did you lose a beacon on Buzz One Four?*
Cleveland: *Yes, I, ah, I haven't painted him since about seven miles south of J thirty-four.*
Washington: *Why don't you transmit? Maybe he hears you.*

As Buzz One Four approached Meyersdale, PA, it staggered to stay aloft in the center of the storm. But the 167 mph winds forced the plane to rocket up and down until an audible 'thud' shook the plane. The aircraft banked hard to the left as the giant tail suddenly tore loose from the empennage[5]. The tail sheared off into the darkness and took with it the left horizontal stabilizer and the gunner's turret section[6].

Without the tail and back left-wing, the aircraft pitched downwards. The pilots lost control of the aircraft, and it spiraled and then rolled over like an animal in the throes of death. In military language, they were now in Negative G, or essentially flying upside down.

Outside, bomber pieces, mainly from the back end of the fuselage[7], were wrenched loose and flew off into the void of the night.

Copilot Peedin turned to McCormick. "God, can you believe this?"

Sergeant Wooten gripped his ejection seat; fear etched deeply across his face. He tried to remember what his training had been for ejecting during a storm. Storms, yes. Blizzards? Did they ever even mention that scenario?

Major Payne touched his pocket with the lucky silver dollar inside, minted in 1944, the year he and Fay had married. He said a silent prayer as he quickly calculated the very real possibility of ejection into a blizzard.

Major Townley had needed to use the urinal right before the turbulence hit and now frantically tried to climb back into his seat and safety harness. "Oh, God, help me!" But everything was chaos.

Major McCormick determined that the plane was no longer navigable. Although he knew the perils of ejecting at such a high altitude, there was no other choice. He reached with his right hand for the alarm and barked out the command, "Bail out, bail out, bail out!"

As each crew member pulled their ejection handles, hatches opened, shoulder harnesses locked, heavy straps clamped around their ankles, and leg supports released. Heads moved back against the headrests for support. The last step was to pull the trigger, which activated the rocket-powered ejection seat.

The entire time from pulling the handle to exiting the bomber would be three seconds.

The first escape hatch to blow was Melvin Wooten's. It blew upward, and immediately all the oxygen and any semblance of warmth sucked itself out of the plane, replaced by brutal howling arctic air of -45°. The electrical circuits went dead, and the men were now on their own in complete darkness. Anything not fastened down flew out through the open escape hatch.

If all went well, and with the plane upside down, Townley and Payne should eject upward from the Black Hole, and McCormick and Peedin <u>would discharge</u> in a downward motion, like Wooten. Four of the men

5 - Back section of the plane
6 - The horizontal stabilizer is the back left wing
7 - Middle part of the plane

ejected out into the frigid glacial sky. Attached to their ejection seats, they entered the air at the same speed the plane had been traveling before they ejected, approximately 500 miles per hour. With zero visibility in the middle of the storm and substantial wind shears, it was like being slammed against a brick wall.

Major Townley was still struggling to reach his ejection seat.

Even with supplemental oxygen, the sub-zero frigid air slashed like a knife through the ejected men's lungs. The searing cold would freeze any exposed skin. Blinded by the blizzard, they could not see beyond their iced face shields.

They had bailed out at 30,000 feet altitude, with parachutes designed to deploy at 12,000 feet. For the 18,000 feet in between, the men were in the stark terror of precipitous free fall, plummeting and tumbling toward the earth while shards of ice blasted their bodies.

Not sky-diving; this was free fall, attached to a tubular metal seat, where you hold on for dear life.

The ejection time registered at 1:38 am, and each man on his own, prayed that his ejection seat would fall away at 14,000 feet, as it was supposed to. Then a prayer for the parachute to automatically deploy at 12,000 feet and the airman to reach 10,000 feet when supplemental oxygen was no longer needed.

The final prayer— land safely.

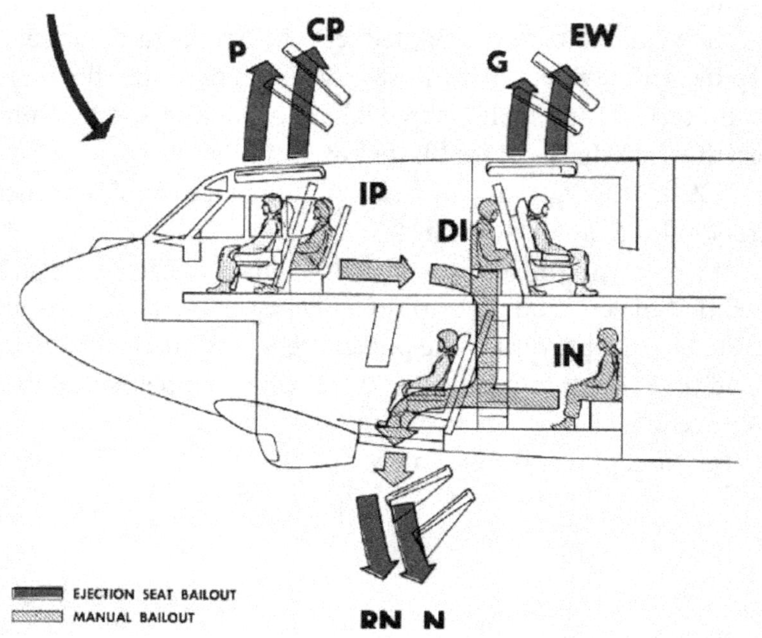

This shows the traditional positions of a B-52 G/H crew and their ejection trajectories: P = Pilot, CP = Copilot, G = Gunner, IN =Instructor (not on Buzz One Four), DI = Bombardier, EW = Electronic War Officer. Buzz One Four was a B-52D, and the gunner position was in the tail. Photo courtesy of B-52: Stratofortress Illustrated, by Lou Drendel.

Monday, January 13, 1964
Temperature, Grantsville, Maryland: 11° F

As the men plummeted downward, now slowed to 120 miles per hour through the shrieking storm, they had no idea of their exact location.

They were heading toward Garrett County, Maryland, 760 miles north from the Turner Air Base's safety. And Garrett County was in the grips of the most gruesome winter blizzard in over 100 years. As the men hurtled through the sky, Buzz One Four was careening on its own path at 500 miles an hour, with the potential of crashing anywhere in the local mountains – or towns.

Lying in western Maryland, Garrett's boundaries include Pennsylvania on the North, West Virginia on the west and south, and Allegany County, Maryland, to the east.

Today, measuring 656 square miles, with an estimate of 20,900 people, Garrett County is still quite rural. The terrain of high mountains, dense forests, and few significant roads makes Garrett the least touched county in Maryland.

With its 29 mountains and seven state forests, it may come as no surprise that Garrett gets more snow than any other county in Maryland. To be precise, during the 1960s, it averaged a yearly snowfall of 110 inches, or 9 feet of snow.

While their families were back in 55-degree weather in Georgia, the Buzz One Four crew dropped out of the sub-zero sky to ground weather biting 11 degrees and a snowstorm that prevented any visibility. They were falling toward Meadow Mountain, which already had more than two feet of snow and new precipitation continuing by the hour. This area was some of the roughest terrains in Garrett County.

Of course, the men had no idea either about the historical significance of the area. Nor did they know they were falling toward the vicinity of Route 40 and Meadow Mountain, 4.5 miles east of Grantsville, Maryland.

The Cleveland Air Traffic Controller sat baffled. The last transmission from Buzz One Four had been so garbled. What had gone wrong? And Washington had had no contact with Buzz One Four either.

The controller made a direct call to Command Post at Westover Air Force Base in Massachusetts.

Cleveland: Westover, are you aware that you have a possible…

Westover: A possible what?

The controller did not want to say "Broken Arrow." He feared it. In military terminology, Broken Arrow describes an accident involving nuclear weapons without the risk of nuclear war. This term also includes incidents in which a nuclear weapon is lost, stolen, or inadvertently detonated.

According to the US military, nuclear weapons have the most secure interlock system of any device, preventing them from accidental detonation and massive destruction.

After all, no one wants a nuclear accident to happen in their neighborhood.

In a farmhouse nestled on the border by Garrett and Allegany, Jesse and Frances Green awoke with a start. Both had been pulled from sleep when a thunderous roar exploded over their home a little before 2:00 a.m. Living near Elbow Mountain's base, where Swamp Road and Westernport Road intersect, Mr. and Mrs. Green anxiously looked at each other.

"What was that?"

"I don't know."

Jesse ran to the window and looked out as a massive airplane barely cleared the roof of their house.

Grabbing coats, both Jesse and Frances ran to the front door and stepped out on the porch. There in the middle of the blizzard, the sky appeared to have turned blood red. An additional sound of crashing thunder and a monstrous flash of fire lit up the sky.

They huddled together.

"You think that came from the plane?"

Then came a monstrous explosion.

"Jesse, we should call the state police."

"Go ahead, Frances, you make the call."

Rose Schriver was still up around 1:50 a.m. when the sound of a giant whoosh sounded behind her house near Lonaconing, Maryland.

Rose's husband was on the cat-eye shift at the Kelly Springfield plant in Cumberland and working night crew until 7 a.m. All five of Rose's children were asleep in their beds, but Rose was awake.

Peering out the back window, she stared at a sky that should be dark, but even in the current raging snowstorm had suddenly turned blood red. In the next instant, the sky went dark again.

Rose wondered if it could be the end of the world. Looking out the window once more toward George's Creek, the snowstorm had obliterated any visibility beyond 30 yards.

She stayed up the rest of the night, checking in on her kids and turning the radio to 105.3 WFRB Frostburg, hoping to get any news. Daylight, and her husband's return, couldn't come soon enough.

Just a few miles away, Allen Ray Broadwater, 16 years old, was out in the barn helping his father check on lambs ready to be born. All of a sudden, a tremendous roar tore across the sky. Neither Allen nor his father knew what to make of it.

With the temperature at 8 degrees, they hurried back to the house. Once on the porch, a new sound like an explosion shattered the night sky. "Might be an airplane," said Allen's father.

As scary as the explosion sounded, the locals had no idea that a B-52 bomber carrying two 9-mega-ton hydrogen bombs would crash nearby.

Nor did they know the B-52 crash had the potential of being catastrophic. If detonated, each bomb had the destructive power of 9 million tons of TNT. The bomb dropped over Hiroshima in World War II only carried the equivalent of 15 thousand tons of TNT.

The airmen still hurtled through the frozen air.

Mack Peedin tumbled over and over into an endless void. He flung out one arm then the other in a desperate attempt to right his body.

Tom McCormick pulled his ripcord prematurely, even though it was designed to deploy on its own. The momentum jerked his body so hard; every bone felt bruised.

The other men were also plummeting, somewhat disoriented, and adrenalin was pumping through their veins.

It would take approximately 80 seconds before the other chutes opened.

Each of those eighty seconds passes like an eternity when plunging through a raging blizzard toward earth at 120 miles an hour. The men could see nothing. Thousands of ice shards pelted them in air so cold they struggled to breathe.

But within 8 minutes, one by one, the crew made contact with the ground in a north-south trajectory, mostly within the Savage River Forest of Garrett County.

Melvin Wooten had been the first to eject and also the first to land.

When his ejection seat shot up and out of the plane, a large piece of jagged metal ripped through his flight suit and broke his thigh bone. Another part of loose metal slashed his face, causing extreme lacerations and bleeding.

Gasping for breath when he landed in a snow-deep field on the outskirts of Salisbury, Pennsylvania, he grimaced as agonizing pain wracked his body.

Cutting himself loose from his parachute and seeing Salisbury's dim lights ahead, he decided to head for the lights. The pain from his broken leg tore through him like a burning saber, and he fell to the ground. Determined to survive, he crawled through the two-foot-high snow toward the town.

In the blinding darkness, he could not see the Casselman River lying directly in his path.

Tom McCormick landed next, approximately two and a half miles south of Melvin Wooten. He had tumbled through the frigid air at a frightening speed but had had the presence of mind to take a compass reading on the lights of Grantsville.

When he accidentally deployed his parachute early, it had also slowed his forward momentum. This action may have been advantageous because he landed not in the middle of the densely wooded Savage River Forest but further north on Meadow Mountain. Striking a dead tree trunk as he landed, bruised even more but grateful to be alive, he reached for his emergency knife attached to his flight suit.

Once he cut himself loose from his parachute, he checked his body for broken bones. Finding none, but realizing the continuing falling snow would only make travel more difficult, he used his parachute for shelter and hunkered down till daylight.

Shaking, he tried to concentrate on anything except the extreme cold.

He pulled up the image of family dinners and his mother's fried biscuits with gravy and potatoes. But that only brought on stomach rumblings. Reaching for the nut bar from his emergency kit, he chewed it slowly to make it last.

The snow obliterated all other sounds, which was possibly a good thing as he wondered if bears and wolves roamed this area. No, the animals would have the sense to stay inside their dens and not venture out into the wrathful force of Mother Nature.

Even the birds are smart enough to only fly in clear weather.

Mack Peedin checked his USAF issued watch; it registered 1:42 am, and then he hit the uppermost branches of a small tree and landed about four miles south of Major McCormick. If he had kept drifting east, he might have hit nearby overhead power lines. His memory of his boy scout days plus his training as an Air Force Pilot made him choose to stay put.

With almost frozen fingers, he pried himself loose from the parachute and dropped to the ground with the chute and his emergency kit.

His kit also contained an inflatable life raft, a sleeping bag, some MREs, a bottle of water, and a fishing hook and line[1]. With great effort, he inflated the life raft and put it down under the sleeping bag. This action at least gave him some insulation from the snow.

He built a small fire and then climbed into the bag and zippered it.

Too drained now even to eat, his body gave way to exhaustion, and he fell asleep.

Major Payne faced a more significant problem when he landed. His parachute tethered itself 30 feet high in a tree in a remote area of Big Savage, further south from Mack Peedin. It took all Payne's strength to cut himself loose and plunge to the ground, completely depleted of energy and now slightly disoriented about his location.

Looking up, he saw his emergency kit still attached to his parachute, dangling in the high branches. Payne did not have the strength or where-with-all to climb up and attempt to retrieve it.

Almost frozen in his thin warm-weather flight jacket, Payne told himself he had to get moving, no matter how difficult. His only chance for survival was to walk out of the forest and find help. Otherwise, he would freeze to death.

Major Townley was still strapped inside the plane.

---

1 - An MRE is a Meal Ready to Eat, and toilet paper is included!

A metal ejection seat from Buzz One Four. It is believed to have been Melvin Wooten's. The men were strapped to their seat until their parachutes automatically deployed. This seat was found miles from where the plane finally crashed. Photo by Linda Sittig, courtesy of the Frostburg Museum.

Monday, January 13, 1964

Buzz One Four collided with Earth on the western slope of Big Savage Mountain. The elevation here is 2,788 feet, approximately eight miles south of Route 40 and directly west of Lonaconing, Maryland. The tail landed first in the state forest by Green Lantern Road, and the bulk of the plane crashed further south near the intersection of Westernport Road and Pine Swamp Road.

Around 4 am, the ring of the front doorbell awakened each of the wives at Turner. Peering out their front windows, each woman held her breath. No one wants the Base Commander to appear in the middle of the night. Hearts pounding, they opened the door.

Something had gone wrong. Did the easy retrieval mission run into trouble?

The Base Commander informed them that the Turner crew had lost all contact around 1:40 a.m. and had presumably crashed somewhere in south-central Pennsylvania. At this point, they considered the five men as missing.

The accompanying Chaplain offered condolences and asked each wife if she would like him to pray.

None of the women objected.

After they left, Dorismarie McCormick lit a cigarette and tried to calm her nerves. Then she recalled the promise Tom had made to her years ago. If he had to bail out of his plane, somehow, somewhere, he would get to a phone and call her.

"Of course," he had joked, "if I bail, I might have to call you collect."

She was determined not to give up and wait instead for his call. But her hands trembled as she dialed Dianne Peedin for any additional details.

Fay Payne continued biting her lip after the Base Commander and Chaplain left. Why hadn't she insisted that Bob find a winter flight-jacket?

Gene Townley's face turned ashen, and her stomach clenched. She couldn't help feeling a sense of dread.

Carol Wooten swallowed her anxiety. Melvin simply had to be alive. She couldn't face raising their three young children without him.

By 4 a.m., the Maryland State Police, alerted by Frances Green, called both the Air Force and the local Army Reserves Unit, advising them about the crash's approximate location.

Before daybreak, Jesse Green dressed in heavy overalls and his thick winter jacket. Tucking leather gloves in his pocket and wearing both a toboggan hat and a tie-down cap, he pulled on his snow boots and left the house.

Within minutes sweat poured off him with the effort it took to trudge through the two-plus feet of snow between his house and his neighbors, John Babe and Effie Layton. But he pushed on until he reached the Layton cabin, and then he and John Babe began the arduous trek to where they assumed the plane had gone down.

"John, what if it's a commercial flight filled with passengers?"

"Pray to God, not."

Slogging through the densely packed snow took more time than they had envisioned. The world became eerily quiet, an arctic landscape of blinding white with no other humans in sight. At 42, Jesse, accustomed to heavy work, found it difficult to breathe as he fought the bitter air and slow-moving progress. Although less than a mile away, it took the two men over an hour to hike across Westernport Road and see the wreckage in the distance.

When they finally approached the plane, he and John Babe stopped, overwhelmed emotionally by the immense devastation before them, their hearts pounding from the exertion.

The gigantic plane, broken now into twisted pieces of fuselage and wings, lay beached on the ground. Massive piles of debris 30 feet high lay everywhere, accompanied by multiple fires.

Nearby stately oaks and pines stood with their top branches sheared off when the aircraft tore through them. It also appeared that the plane had gouged out a 75-yard-long crater before it came to rest. In total, a 1,000-foot path of destruction had forced itself across the west slope of Big Savage Mountain.

Obvious to Jesse and John Babe, there could not have been any survivors.

The two men could smell the sickening odor of jet fuel, but Jesse wanted to get closer to the plane. An Air Force reconnaissance team would arrive soon, and the entire area would be off-limits. But the fires and the intense heat held him back.

Stunned by the tragedy, Jesse put his hands in his pockets and just stared at the mountain of wreckage as the snow started to fall once more and pile up over the debris.

He and John Babe were utterly unaware that the two thermonuclear bombs lay only 50 feet from them, still intact.

Two relatives of Allen Broadwater, Robert and Stanley Warnick, arrived at the Broadwater farm shortly after daybreak with the plane crash announcement. As Allen and his father suited up to investigate, they found a large section of an airplane wing had landed next to their barn, laying against the barn wall.

And even more surprising was the sheep who had gathered under the shelter of the wing to get out from the still falling snow.

They pushed through the snow and realized it would be near im-possible to make any progress. So, Stanley Warnick went back home, got a horse, and let the horse blaze a trail through the snow to the crash site.

Finally arriving, they discovered Jesse Green and John Babe Layton already there. Exploded pieces of the airplane wreckage, tires, wheels, and sections of the fuselage were scattered everywhere.

Allen looked at the crater the plane had gouged out of the Earth. Twenty-five feet deep, it bore testimony to the power of the impact.

Near where the local men stood, two nuclear bombs sat beneath the wreckage. Two Army men approached, one of them carrying a Geiger counter. One man took a wand and passed it over Allen's body, then his father's, and then both Warnick's, checking for signs of radiation. However, due to the extreme weather, the readings were not reliable. Later, Allen and his father learned that one of the bombs had a small crack.

Even though the crash had occurred in Garrett County, Lonaconing, Maryland in Allegany County, lay closest to the crash site.

Lonaconing is a small town of only .36 square miles and, in the 1960s, had a population of 2,000 people. Before its involvement in the rescue ef-forts for the B-52 crash, Lonaconing had three notable achievements: coal mines, a silk factory, and the hometown of Lefty Grove, a famous baseball player for the Philadelphia Athletics and Boston Red Sox.

Bob Foote of Lonaconing, had been plowing snow with his partner Emerson Alexander since 6 a.m. on Sunday. It was a never-ending process because the snow continued to fall, and Route 40, the main connector road, was a mess.

By nightfall Sunday, they had plowed and replowed the main road several times for the state roads department. Hours into the night, they passed the popular Happy Hills Farms Restaurant and the Stonehenge Bar along the Route 40 Long Stretch when the sky shook with a tremendous thunderclap.

"What was that?"

Bob shrugged. "Maybe, thundersnow?" It wasn't unusual for thunder to boom out of the mountains during a blizzard. They both looked up, but a continuous sheet of white snow blanketed the entire sky.

Only two miles south of Long Stretch, Buzz One Four's vertical stabilizer had just slammed upright into the ground off Green Lantern Road.

By 4 a.m. Monday, they were still at work plowing with their yellow four-wheel-drive Tractioneer when they received a radio call from their supervisor. A plane had crashed, and they were to return to the county road garage on the far west side of Frostburg, near Savage Mountain. "Fuel up, chain every wheel, load with salt, and meet state trooper Milt Hart at the traffic light in Lonaconing," were their instructions.

That thunder last night? Perhaps it had been a plane, mused Bob.

Twenty-two hours into this incredibly long shift, Bob was grateful he'd packed enough food. He had a thermos of hot tea and six bologna sandwiches—Frostburg bologna, famous throughout the area from Engle's Butcher Shop.

Bob and Emerson made their way from Frostburg down Route 36 to Lonaconing to meet the state police. Their huge 5-ton yellow truck had a wing plow on either side. The plow on the front could clear up to ten feet, and the side plows could each do six. No wonder it took two men to man the truck. While Emerson drove the Tractioneer, Bob operated the side plows.

The two men started up Douglas Avenue in Lonaconing, just off Route 36, and drove out past the Lonaconing Forestry Boys Camp, heading for Swamp Road. Milt Harte had given them directions, but not the wreck's exact location.

The time ticked slowly while the two men inched their way west from Lonaconing over to Big Savage Mountain.

As they made their way left on Swamp Road, they encountered two

Maryland State Troopers with their vehicle stuck in the snow. Using shovels and their plow, Bob and Emerson helped the men get their patrol car back onto the Westernport road.

Meanwhile, the snow continued to fall.

Finally, hours after they started, they reached their destination off Pine Swamp Road. Bob and Emerson then spied Jesse Green and John Babe Layton standing at the top of the hill, peering down on Harry Russell's timber property.

Bob had helped log that timber property three years ago, working with a team of horses to transport the logs. Who would have thought he would be here again, but this time plowing through a blizzard?

After Bob and Emerson finished plowing, Asa Wilhelm ran the Garrett County Roads Department grader to keep the road clear.

It would be an additional 11 hours before Bob and Emerson finally stopped, making it a 33-hour shift.

During that time frame, Milt Harte, the Maryland State Trooper, and his son, would climb up on what they thought was a part of an engine. Milt wanted to get a better view of the destruction. But he inadvertently had climbed up on one of the bombs.

John Ravenscroft had risen early and made it to Lonaconing to get a paper by 6 a.m. While he paid for it, a policeman came and alerted John about the plane crash.

John went home, got his brother Robert and his brother-in-law, Roy Lambert. They intended to go to the site and see it for themselves.

When they finally arrived, State Police had set up a perimeter, and a few other residents climbed through the snow to inspect the crash. John's gaze moved up to what looked like tin roping strung along the tree's upper branches.

Looks like Christmas decorations, he mused.

Later he would learn that the 'tin foil' was chaff or thin strips of aluminum. Chaff acts as a decoy, and when deployed by the EWO (electronic weapons officer), it appears as scattered missile targets on enemy radar screens. The plane's explosion had released all 1,000 pounds of chaff, which now hung in strips over the winter oaks, maples, and pines of Big Savage Mountain. Wiring from the plane lay strewn all over the ground.

John managed to climb on the part of one wing, only to have an Air Force Military Policeman holding an M-30 caliber carbine motion to John to get off. Now.

John complied but intended to come back later.

Harold Nicol served with the Army Reserves Military Police based in Lonaconing, Maryland. Asleep alongside his wife Helen, a noise like a ferocious train crash woke him. Peering out the window, the whiteness of the waist-high snow glistened back at him, and still more flakes fell.

He nodded back to sleep only to be awakened by the jangle of the phone. Captain Chaney of the Maryland State Police needed him.

"Harold, I need you to take a three-quarter-ton truck and go help George Kirkwood with the city police (Lonaconing). Can you drive a tractor-trailer?"

"Ah, no, well, maybe, if I had to." Harold rubbed the sleep from his eyes.

"Been a plane crash. There's a chemical team arriving, and even with four-wheel drive, everyone's going to have trouble getting through. We need a team that can get up Swamp Road, and I need you to leave ASAP."

Harold quickly dressed, stopping only for a cup of coffee and some toast. Then he left to join a first responders team heading to the crash site.

After Harold left, his wife Helen had no idea of when he might return. She worried that he hadn't taken any extra food with him. Not able to do anything about that, Helen got up and went to the basement to stoke and bank the coal furnace so the house would be warm. Then she tended to their 3-month-old baby and started breakfast.

The snow had drifted all night, making many roads impassable. Harold's team drove as far as they could, then got out and walked. They found snow fences, installed to keep snow off the thoroughfares, buried in the drifts. In the still winter air, the men heard the commotion up ahead, so they had to be near the crash site.

Arriving at the scene, Harold stared with disbelief at the devastation in front of him. The plane debris covered every inch of ground and looked like a twisted aluminum mountain. Trees were down on all the hillsides, and the pungent smell of jet fuel mingling with burnt hardwoods soaked the air.

Then, Milt Hart of the State Police came over and told Harold's team to be careful where they walked. But no one mentioned the bombs, still lying in the nearby debris.

As Harold got closer to the wreckage, a small door suddenly popped open, and a pair of Air Force boots fell out. Harold's eyebrows arched. Good Lord, what else might fall out of there? But nothing did.

As the day went on, Harold and his group assisted other teams helping the phone company. Emergency phone lines were needed to communicate with the Air Force, Maryland State Police, and rescue crews. The military police strung up lines on trees. And one line had to be explicitly reserved for the Pentagon.

The hours zinged by. Well into the afternoon, Harold's stomach let loose an audible growl. He looked sheepishly at a young state policeman standing next to him. "Sorry, I haven't eaten all day."

In a gesture that would come to define all of the community who turned out to help, the patrolman didn't hesitate. "Here, I've got a cheese sandwich; I'll split it with you." And the two men gratefully ate their halves, a blessing since the Red Cross did not arrive until 10 p.m. with food for the responder teams.

Harold wished he had asked the young patrolman his name. Fifty-six years later, Harold Nicol and former state trooper Dick Graham confirmed via a telephone call to each other that Dick had split his cheese sandwich with Harold, those many years ago.

And Harold Nicol was finally able to thank Dick Graham for that generous act.

When the Maryland State Troopers first reached the crash site, they too, like Jesse Green, silently gaped in horror at the scene in front of them. But unlike Jesse Green, the troopers had been alerted that a recon team had left Andrews Air Force Base outside of Washington, DC, and headed this way, anxious to reach the destination and assess the situation.

In addition to worrying about the missing five-man crew, the Air Force had a more pressing problem confronting them: Buzz One Four's nuclear bombs.

To that avail, a 15-man unit, the 28th Ordnance Disposal Team from Fort Meade, Maryland, had been assigned to secure the bombs. Bill Ramsey headed the bomb disposal squad, grateful for the Maryland State Police escort that brought them to the crash site. Peering around, he spied some civilians roaming through the area on snowshoes. He was also glad that Carl Ellenburg would be the guy to deactivate the explosives. Then the team would keep watch throughout Monday night until the bombs were secured.

To help, the Maryland State Troopers would maintain a 24-hour roadblock to keep all unauthorized personnel from going near the crash. By 9 am, the Troopers had constructed a 1,500-foot radial perimeter fence around the crash site.

By nightfall, the crash had generated rescue efforts by the Maryland State Troopers, the Fort Meade Ordnance Team, the Maryland State Roads Commission, the Civil Air Patrol, the Military Police of the Army Reserves, the National Guard, the C & P Telephone Company, the US Department of Forestry, the Pennsylvania State Police, the US Army, and of course, the US Air Force.

By Tuesday, January 14th, over 100 residents, mostly untrained in rescue maneuvers, would come forward to volunteer in the search for survivors. They had what the military did not: a life-long knowledge of the land and the mountains. By the end of the week, their numbers would significantly increase.

This photo was taken days after the crash. The density and isolation of the forest is evident by the way the four-story tail is wedged in the trees. Photo courtesy of www. salisburypa.com/b52crash.html .

This photo was taken in 1947 in Alaska when famous aviator Charles Lindbergh requested that Tom McCormick be his co-pilot on a test run. Photo courtesy of Matt McCormick, grandson of Tom McCormick.

Monday, January 13, 1964

Tom McCormick awoke Monday morning and stared out on the vast expanse of the snow-covered landscape all around him. His entire body ached like he had been beaten, and he would have loved just to lay down until a rescue team arrived.

But his location might not be determined for days, and that prospect did not sit well with him. Using his compass and calculating the high terrain, he followed survival rules to start walking to a lower elevation, where he could find adequate shelter and, hopefully, a farmhouse.

He had no idea that he was at the top of the Meadow Mountain, north of Route 40 and several miles east of Grantsville. The area's nickname? The Maryland Alps.

The wind whistled down the steep slopes of Meadow Mountain as he forged into the snow. He shivered and reminisced about when he flew a B-17 in Alaska with Charles Lindbergh. *I survived flying with Lindbergh; I'll survive this, too.*

Mack Peedin awoke 4 miles south of Thomas McCormick and poked his head out of his rigged sleeping tent. The biting cold slapped him in the face, and he ducked back in his crudely constructed emergency shelter, out of the brutal elements. Hoping that his bright yellow parachute should be easy to spot from a rescue plane, he decided not to leave his shelter.

Now out of the sleeping bag, he ate another MRE. It couldn't match the memory of his grandmother's fried chicken, but he was grateful to have any food. Then to keep his blood circulating, he rubbed his hands together. Peering out into the frozen panorama of trees covered in snow, he looked at the low hanging clouds. *Just my luck; more snow on the way. Not even a bird in the sky.* He figured his chances were still better if he stayed put.

Well before dawn, Melvin Wooten grimaced in agony. He could see town lights ahead of him. Oh God, he had crawled so far and still not close enough to be seen by a rescue team. Nearly frozen, he forced himself to keep going. The alternative would mean certain death.

With the predawn icy wind blowing around him and 11-degree weather causing the ice to rim his face, he continued to drag himself through the snow. Each movement tore pain through his body, but he gritted his teeth and kept inching forward.

Major Payne was freezing, literally. Because of his inadequate clothing and lack of access to his emergency kit, he had wandered off down one trail and then another with only a few emergency items in his pockets. He had stayed put for an hour after he landed but then left well before daybreak.

The weather did not cooperate. No matter which way he moved, the snow continued to hamper both his progress and his visibility. He kept turning his head, first one way, then another, hoping or expecting to find the right path to safety.

The hours wore on into the predawn morning as he lumbered through the snow. Then he would stop, and confused, begin on a different path. The extreme cold affected his mind, and he became more disoriented.

His tracks in the snow indicated that he had doubled back over steps he had already taken, but his mind could not sort out that fact. No food, thin outer gear, and shock from the frigid weather were all combatting to make him weaker and weaker. Nevertheless, he continued his frantic push through the snow, his breathing becoming more labored with each step.

By 4 p.m., Tom McCormick struggled. He had left his shelter six hours earlier and had trekked non-stop through thigh-high snow in his effort to reach the lower ground. Mountain peaks surrounded him everywhere he looked, and once he managed to hike out of one section of forest, another dense thicket of trees, rocks, and boulders thwarted his forward progress.

Not sure I can keep on going. No, don't stop. Take just a few more steps.

His face, frozen by ice, matched the sensation of no feeling in his fingers or toes. Frostbite had set in.

Pushing through the trees, almost stumbling, he finally came out on the western side of a mountain to what might have been a meadow. His eyes stung from the cold, and he rubbed them. Peering intently ahead and wondering if snowscapes can cause a mirage, he spied what he prayed was the outline of a barn. It would turn out to be the Warnick barn.

Robert Warnick was renting Stone House Farm about 3 miles east of Grantsville and 10 miles north from where Buzz One Four had crashed.

Ten-year-old Daniel Warnick had the day off from school in Grantsville due to the blizzard. As Daniel peered out the kitchen window late in the afternoon, he joked with his father, wondering if any of the missing

The approximate area where Tom McCormick walked out of the woods, six hours after trekking 2 1/4 miles through thigh high snow. Photo by Linda Sittig.

crewmen could be in the woods near their house.

Daniel squinted. "Dad, I think I see someone out on the edge of the north pasture."

"Not in this snow, you don't."

"Yeah, Dad. I do. There's a guy out there."

Robert Warnick looked out the window, surprised.

"C'mon, son. Grab a jacket and boots. We need to go see who it might be."

Now, who in their right mind would be out in this weather?

Robert and Daniel walked through their shoveled path to the barn. They could see the man, way off to their right, wobbling against the snow.

Robert calculated they had only an hour before the sunset, and he certainly did not want to be outside in the dark.

Father and son set off, making a narrow path through the field and worried that the man might collapse before they reached him. Robert waved, and the man feebly raised his arm in return. Finally, they were within earshot. Robert yelled, "Are you lost?"

The man replied in a raspy voice, "Not now."

Tom McCormick stopped at the farm fence; even if he wanted to, he didn't have the strength to climb over it. Robert and Daniel worked together to help Tom maneuver the obstacle. Then they supported Tom back to the farmhouse.

Kathleen Warnick looked up in surprise from their fieldstone house when the door flew open. Her husband came in half-dragging, half-holding a man covered in snow and appearing to be in a severely weakened state.

After they got McCormick to a chair, Kathleen started a concoction of hot coffee laced with warm milk and told McCormick to sip it slowly.

Tom's fingers were so cramped he had trouble holding onto the cup.

Daniel came over and offered to loosen the man's boots so his feet could warm up. But the laces were frozen stiff, and it took a tremendous effort to remove the Air Force boots. When Daniel peeled off Tom's socks, he could see that the feet had hardly any circulation, so he gently rubbed them.

Tom nodded. "Thank you. But I need to make a phone call."

Over 760 miles away, the phone rang in the McCormick's house at Turner. Neighbors and friends had spent hours there, offering support. Now, Dorismarie rushed to pick up the receiver.

"Hello?"

"I have a collect call from a Thomas McCormick. Will you accept the charge?"

Dorismarie sank into a chair, tears streaming down her face. "Yes, of course, I will."

As night fell, Joseph Stakem of the Maryland State Police escorted Tom McCormick to Memorial Hospital in Cumberland. Tom carried the hope that the rest of his crew had also made it to safety.

Dorismarie called Dianne Peedin. But no one had any news about Dianne's husband or the other men. This was the longest day Dorismarie could ever remember.

It had been a long day for the Maryland State Troopers as well. Ray Andrews had been coming off his second shift when he got the early morn-

The Warnick farmhouse in 2020. After his two and a quarter mile trek through the snow, Tom McCormick found food and shelter with the Warnick family. Photo by Linda Sittig.

ing phone call. Milt Harte told Ray to get some extra warm clothes and suit up, then head out of Lonaconing to the crash site.

Ray already had the chains on his '63 Ford Police Cruiser, which gave him the traction he needed on the snowy roads. When he reached the top of Savage Mountain, he noticed Milt off talking with someone. Ray parked his car and climbed over the big snow mound in front of him. Only later did he realize it was a 4-foot snow fence. But the drifts had been so big, he never even touched the fencing.

Ray spent most of that Monday ferrying military personnel from the VFW in Lonaconing up the crash site.

About 9:30 p.m., Ray tuckered out. He had climbed the hill north of Swamp Road and glanced over at a section of the fuselage when he spied a light inside. Going over to investigate, he found a guy dressed in heavy Arctic winter gear and a fur-lined parka sitting in the fuselage, eating a meal.

"Hey, who are you?" Ray asked.

"I'm with the Air Force. Don't worry. They sent me down here to guard the remains of the plane throughout the night.

"Well, where did you come from?" Ray wanted to know.

"Greenland," the man answered.

"Greenland?"

"Yes, sir, I'm trained to deal with icy terrain."

"OK, then. I'll keep going." Ray marveled to himself. *Greenland? Well, didn't that beat all?*

Army driver Jay L. Atkins and Carroll Sampson retrieved this army vehicle called a weasel in Cumberland, Maryland. A weasel is an off-track hybrid vehicle with the top half resembling a jeep, and the bottom part contains the continuous tracks of a tank. It may not be pretty, but it gets you where you need to go .Atkins and Sampson drove it to Garrett County for help with the rescue mission. Along the way an axle broke and the weasel had to be towed to the Jenkins barn for repairs. Photo courtesy of the Grantsville Museum.

Day Three

January 14, 1964

Major Robert E. Townley – Bombardier of Buzz One Four, age 42, from Gadsden, Alabama. Photo courtesy of BuzzOneFour.org.

7

Tuesday, January 14, 1964
Temperature, Grantsville, Maryland: 16° F

Sterling Queen relished the small amount of sleep from last night.

Yesterday started when the phone rang in the wee hours of the morning. Still at home, in Terra Alta, West Virginia, he learned a plane had crashed over in Garrett County, Maryland. A B-52, to be exact, and his unit of the Civil Air Patrol needed to assist in the security effort.

As a part of the US Air Force and Commander of the Clarksburg, West Virginia unit, Sterling would need to assemble a 10-man team and get to the crash site as soon as possible. Their job would be to protect the two nuclear bombs from anyone other than authorized military personnel.

"You are authorized to use deadly weapons, if necessary," his superior told him. Sterling told his men to bring carbines.

The raging winter blizzard from Sunday and Monday had grounded all planes, and his crew would have to drive to the crash site. Dressed in heavy overalls and winter flight suits, his team assembled in the dark and began their trek to Garrett County, Maryland. According to his calculations, the crash site would be an 85-mile trip. The drive was tricky in any weather but treacherous on roads covered from blizzard conditions with near-zero temperatures.

Their Jeeps headed east toward Oakland, Maryland. And from there to Route 136 at the southern tip of the Savage River State Forest. The trip could take two hours in summer, but now the snowdrifts of two to three feet deep would hamper their progress.

Finally, coming off Backbone Mountain, Maryland's highest peak, they reached the tiny settlement of Bloomington. Backbone Mountain, at an elevation of 3,360 feet, filled even experienced truckers with dread. Two rows of white crosses on the rock wall stood in remembrance of truck drivers whose runaway trucks had not been able to negotiate the hairpin turn.

Dawn broke as they arrived at the BUZZ ONE FOUR crash site; multiple fires burned everywhere. Fortunately, the National Guard from Cumberland, Maryland, had brought in a weasel for the Civil Air Patrol team to navigate over the rough terrain.

An Army sergeant met them and told them to run off all spectators and confiscate cameras and film.

Sterling looked at the desolation surrounding them. A half-mile of destruction documented that a superstorm had forced a crash that had reduced the largest military aircraft in America to mammoth piles of rubble.

The Civil Air Patrol team went to work, unaware that some civilians had been able to breach the security.

Leo Mills was only ten years old when he went with his father, Brennan Mills, and his uncle, Gene Whetstone, to investigate. The trio had hunted in the backwoods before and could hike up Swamp Road's backside in deep snow. For ten-year-old Leo, the 30 inches of snow went up to his chest, and he had to walk in his father's footsteps.

Soon, they spied a mangled chunk of the plane wreckage that had been in the tail section. Both Brennan and Gene quickly took their Bell and Howell 8mm cameras and filmed the scene. Brennan stashed his camera in the back interior pocket his wife had sewn inside his coat. Gene wasn't so lucky.

Gene was holding his camera when seemingly out of nowhere, two National Guardsmen carrying carbines appeared. "Hand us the camera, now." Leo watched as the guardsman opened his uncle's camera and removed the film. Then Leo, Brennan, and Gene departed.

The guardsmen proceeded to secure the area, confiscating film when they found it. Orders were for civilians to leave the immediate area and not breach the police perimeter. Throughout the morning, responding teams searched for any surviving military items, being sure to remove sensitive documents.

By late afternoon, Sterling Queen had been standing guard by the Pentagon emergency phone for hours. Although dressed in an Arctic parka and wearing muck-lucks, he now worried about frostbite and kept moving his feet to aid circulation.

By night, with no food or rest, the team was grateful when the Red

After the crash, tons of debris were taken to Frostburg, Maryland for later retrieval by the U.S. Air Force. This is a small corner of one such debris pile. Photo courtesy Grantsville Museum.

Cross finally arrived with food. Unfortunately, with the frigid weather, the oatmeal froze in the bowls before they could eat it. Coffee left to set, turned ice-cold within a minute, as the night temperature dipped below zero and the winds picked up to 35 miles per hour.

Sterling worried about his team, but soon he had an idea. The Lonaconing Forestry Boys Camp, located about 4 miles from the crash site, had barracks. Camp might be a misnomer because the boys had been assigned there by the juvenile court. Sterling took a jeep and drove up Lonaconing Road to the center. He asked the director to turn one of the boys' barracks into sleeping quarters for his team. His men desperately needed a few hours of sleep if they were to continue their patrol duties.

With that accomplished, he divided his squad into sleeping shifts and took the time to examine his almost frozen right foot. With massaging and a warm blanket, he prayed that he could avoid the consequence of frostbite.

When he awoke after his three-hour sleep, the snow had finally stopped.

His team quickly got back to work patrolling the crash site, searching for documents, and keeping civilians away from scavenging souvenirs and away from contact with the bombs.

Tuesday morning found the remaining four wives back at Turner, each one thinking of her husband.

Because Melvin Wooten was an airman and not an officer, his wife Carol had never really mingled with the officer's wives. She now sat alone in a chair and peered out the window, praying that the Chaplain's car would not arrive.

Melvin had always been such a sweet guy who made friends quickly. It would not be fair for something bad to happen to him.

She let her mind drift back eight years to when she and Melvin met. He was stationed at Ellsworth Air Force Base outside Rapid City, South Dakota. Petite, pretty, and pert, Carol had gone with her high school friends to the local roller-skating rink on Main Street. Melvin and his Air Force buddies also went skating that night.

Melvin and Carol began to chat, and then he asked her to skate. They were both so young, but with an undeniable attraction between them. They married a few months later, and then he left for California for specialized training while Carol stayed in South Dakota.

The phone rang, bringing Carol out of her memories of the past. She swallowed the fear as she answered—just a neighbor calling for any new information about Melvin.

Dianne Peedin wandered from room to room, performing trivial chores, trying to keep her mind occupied, but with little success.

She turned on their brand new 19-inch Philco TV to Jacqueline Kennedy dressed in widow's black.

Dianne let out a deep sigh. Had it only been seven weeks since the assassination of President John F. Kennedy? She suddenly sensed a kinship to Jackie Kennedy, whose style she had always admired. Dianne mused that the prospect of widowhood is something no woman wants to face but could happen at any given moment.

She watched the news about Jackie and her children and said another prayer that Mack would be found alive.

Gene Townley wished her older son Don was still at home. He'd be a comfort to her right now. Her other son, Reed, at seven, couldn't share with her the terror that beat in her heart. Gene would be turning 40 this year, even though she still looked young with her trim figure and thick wavy chocolate-brown hair. Right now, Gene longed for the comfort that

U.S. Army convoy forming in Grantsville, Maryland, in January 1964. Photo courtesy of Gerry Beachy and BuzzOneFour.org.

only families could provide. But all their relatives resided back in Gadsden, Alabama, which seemed like a million miles away.

Fay Payne stood in the living room of their house in Albany. All she could think of was how Bob would often come home, right at dinner time, and suddenly whirl her around the kitchen as if they were on a dance floor, not taking his eyes off her.

It was part of what she loved most about him, his ability always to make her smile.

They had met when Fay enrolled in business school in Tulsa, Oklahoma, and quickly discovered their shared love of dancing. Throughout their years in the military, they had stayed socially active, attending base dances and other events. At 5 foot 5, Fay delighted in wearing spiky high heels and still did not reach Bob's height.

They each had interests of their own. Fay loved art and would paint, sculpt, or create pottery. Bob enjoyed boats and kept one in a slip at Alligator Point, Florida, a three-hour drive due south to Mexico's Gulf.

Steve Timney, with the 372nd Military Police Unit from Lonaconing, was on his second day of what was hopefully just a three-day shift.

Yesterday, he supervised setting up the VFW Hall basement in Lonaconing with enough cots for the visiting military police called in for security detail. Today, he headed for the crash site with instructions to scout around for military documents or artifacts that needed to be retrieved.

Although the snow had stopped, the back roads were still almost impassable. Steve remembered an old logging road off of Westernport Road. He started in a three-quarter-ton truck but eventually had to switch to a weasel.

At the site, Steve walked the inner perimeter. Destruction lay everywhere, and he wasn't sure he'd find anything. But within a few hours, he sighted an Air Force crash helmet and a battered brown leather briefcase. Two important finds.

Two state troopers, Dick Graham and Milt Hart from the nearby La Vale Station were walking the crash site and inspecting the debris. Near what had been the cockpit, they suddenly stopped. It looked like an Air Force uniform buried under the rubble and snow.

Upon closer inspection, they realized they had found Major Robert Townley's remains, and next to the major's body lay his safety buckles, still unclasped.

Robert Townley had died upon impact when the plane crashed.

Dick and Milt were visibly shaken and commiserated with each other. "Poor guy, he must have been filled with terror as the plane went down."

Milt nodded in agreement. Then Dick and Milt stopped talking, and in the silence, they each wondered what had happened to this man that he had not been able to eject from the aircraft. And where was the rest of the crew?

The discovery of Major Townley shifted the rescue attempts to a sobering reality of the human tragedy involved. The question now loomed as to whether there would be any other survivors.

A phone call went to Turner Air Base, and the Chaplain and Base Commander were soon on their way to Gene Townley's house. No matter how often the Commander made these calls, it never got any easier. One grief-stricken look from the surviving spouse can crumble even the most stalwart of officers.

An hour later, Gene picked up the phone to call Robert's siblings.

When George Townley received the news of his brother's death, he broke down and wept. His two daughters, Gina and Lisa, had never seen their father cry before.

With Tuesday's cleared weather, an air armada of approximately 40 rescue aircraft took to the skies over the Savage River State Forest. Below them were 52,812 acres of heavily wooded terrain, and hopefully three survivors.

Five US Marine and six US Army helicopters flew low while fifteen US Air Force light engine planes scoured from a higher altitude. Private pilots and Pennsylvania and Maryland Civil Air Patrol Units took to the skies as well. Cessnas scanned the rugged hillsides for any signs of the remaining crewmen.

When Mack Peedin awoke Tuesday morning, he peered out of his crude tent shelter. With a sigh of relief that the skies were clear, he prayed that meant no more snow.

He shook last night's snow off the shelter top so any rescue planes could see the bright neon yellow material of his parachute.

Then he sighed: what he wouldn't give for a pack of Marlboro's, or a Jack Daniels. He thought of his wife and young son Charlie. A wave of despair washed over him, but he forced himself not to give in. Despair can quickly turn desolation into desperation.

Gazing out on the frozen landscape around him, he likened himself to a character from a Jack London story, stranded in the Yukon with slim hope of rescue.

Then he talked himself out of that morbid idea. He'd stay put. There would be rescue planes out looking for him; he just had to survive long enough for them to find him.

At least he was on the ground, not hurtling through space like that crazy Russian astronaut, Yuri Gagarin, did three years ago aboard the Vostok 1 Spacecraft.

Mack calculated it had been 30 hours since he ejected. Returning to his survival kit, he took out another MRE, made another small fire, and retrieved the M-6 folded rescue rifle. The gun, intended as protection from wild animals or to hunt for food, could attract attention. Assembling it and loading ammunition, he fired it into the air, hoping that someone would hear it and lead a rescue party to him.

Then he sat back down on the life raft/sleeping bag and ate the small meal.

Hazel Klotz served as the town's news crier, updating the populace hourly regarding the rescue efforts and the weather. A popular Grantsville radio host on WFRB, she used both her organizational talents and the airwaves to alert Garrett County residents of how they could help.

A friendly woman who hosted the local WFRB radio show, "At Home with Hazel," her regular activity shared recipes and homemaking tips for women. And that is how she became the emergency news reporter for updates on the rescue attempts. With all the radio equipment already installed in her home, Hazel gave hourly reports.

Last night Hazel had gone on air: "There's a B-52 down, and everyone needs to keep their porch lights on throughout the night." In that way, she figured, any survivors might use the lights as a beacon to safety. God help those remaining airmen.

As of this morning, there were close to 1,000 people helping in the rescue efforts. When you consider that Grantsville had a population of just over 450 people, the rescue teams more than doubled the number of people in and around Grantsville. The military alone had sent Marines, Army, and Air Force personnel to help in the rescue. One hundred thirty men were bunking at the American Legion building, 152 had cots at the Grantsville Fire Hall, another 150 were sleeping at the Grantsville Elementary School, and 50 men were at the Lutheran Church. Each day, more and more locals were assisting in the rescue search throughout the days and nights.

And that did not even count the volunteer military bivouacked in Lona- coning and at the National Guard Armory on Brown Avenue in Cumberland.

Folks who live on the mountain are a hardy sort. Long ago, they learned the importance of self-reliance and taking care of each other. After the crash occurred, most Garrett people asked, "How can I help?"

To which Hazel replied, "We have to figure out how to feed all these men who are here. We got Maryland State Police, Army, Air Force, Ma- rines, National Guard, and Civil Air Patrol, as well as our neighbors."

How does one start the gargantuan task of feeding over 1,000 volun- teers thrown together in a traumatic situation?

You turn to the ladies of nearby churches. Numerous worship plac- es, including St. John's Lutheran Church in south Cumberland and Christ Lutheran Church in Grantsville, rose to the task.

According to local legend, Hazel rallied the local women to start cooking the meals.

The dinners turned out to be impressive. The women whipped up platters of baked ham, roasted chicken, mashed potatoes, corn, coleslaw, and rolls. The following night they featured stuffed pork chops.

Never had military and civilian volunteers been fed this well. While the ladies cooked, the volunteers sat down next to strangers and filled themselves with food and companionship.

A crew of Pennsylvania Civil Air Patrol pilots maneuvered their helicopters and light planes throughout the skies. Around 1 p.m., one of the pilots sighted a bright yellow spot perched high in the trees. He radioed back that he might have found a survivor.

Mack Peedin heard the plane and jumped up, waving his arms. Even

The Ray Jenkins house in 2020. Mack Peedin was taken here before being airlifted to the Cumberland Hospital after his rescue. Photo by Linda Sittig.

though he couldn't see the pilot, he saw the tail number of "370 Charlie" and prayed the pilot had seen him. Relief washed over Mack, and his knees buckled. Oh, dear God. Thank you.

Within the next hour, Mack greeted his rescuers, who had tramped over a mile through the snow on Ray Jenkins' farm to reach him. "Hey, welcome to my living room," Mack joked even though his hands were shaking.

The rescuers were snow drenched and cold, so Mack told them to hover near his makeshift fire and warm themselves. Finally, the small group plodded back through the snow to the Jenkins' farmhouse. Then, Major Cecil B. Arthur of the Pennsylvania Civil Air Patrol unit transported Mack via helicopter to Cumberland.

The phone rang in Smithfield, N.C., at the home of Charles Britton.

As Mr. Britton picked up the receiver, his daughter's voice came across the line.

"He's safe, Daddy. Mack's alive!"

And the 64-year-old father-in-law of Mack Peedin wiped tears from his eyes.

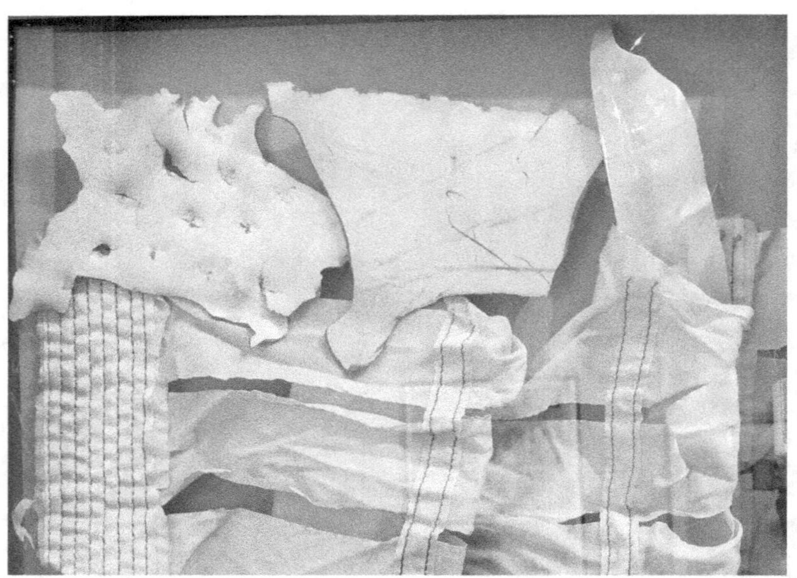

Recovered sections of a parachute from Buzz One Four, but not attributed to any one airman. Photo courtesy of Frostburg Museum. Photo by Linda Sittig.

A steep hill leading down to Poplar Lick. During the rescue mission, this hill would have been covered in three feet of snow. Photo courtesy of Bucky Schriver.

Tuesday, January 14, 1964

Lester Bittinger of Grantsville had been in the small rescue party that walked copilot Mack Peedin the one and a half miles back to Ray Jenkins' home.

The afternoon sun dipped in the west, and Lester pulled his coat collar up around his neck. A warm glow of satisfaction spread through his body with the successful discovery and rescue of the copilot. Now Lester headed home.

He drove down Fairview Road to the section known as the 'back-woods' and turned into his farm lane. The day began to settle, and he walked behind his house and glanced up at the ridge. A few treetops looked like they had been sheared off. He climbed up further to investigate, and when he reached the peak, he looked off to the east and saw a splash of yellow in some trees facing Poplar Lick.

Lester reasoned it could be another parachute. Back at his house, he alerted Harland Upole, the Superintendent at New Germany State Park Headquarters, about his find.

Nineteen-year-old Gary Finzel was at the White Oak Inn, helping his parents, the owners. Men at the bar nodded to each other about the possible parachute sighting. Soon, new volunteers agreed to join a rescue team. While the military officials had planned to use a four-wheel-drive Tractioneer to get the men deep into the forest, the four-foot-high drifts of snow made that too difficult.

The men would have to strike out on foot. At first, the strategy was to organize two teams. One team would enter the terrain from the end of Fairview Road near Lester's farm, and the other team would approach from Savage River Road.

By the time the first rescue team left Fairview Road, the sun had set, and the temperature had dropped below zero. The Savage River Road team, team number two, met with overwhelming obstacles and had to turn back.

It took the Fairview Road team over an hour of forcing their bodies through the Savage River Forest to traverse a mile to reach the location of what did turn out to be a parachute.

The men stood there, gazing toward the top of the tree. Solidly lodged in the uppermost branches hung a bright yellow parachute and emergency kit. Using their flashlights, they glanced around at the ground before them. Tracks went off in multiple directions, and then some doubled back to the base of the tree. It appeared that the airman who crashed with this parachute had struck out more than once, looking for the best trail to safety.

They surmised he adhered to a survival mandate for the mountains, head for lower terrain, and a stream to follow.

But whose parachute? Major Payne or Tech Sergeant Wooten? They couldn't tell, at least not yet.

Walking together, the team followed the most promising trail. No one spoke of the dreaded possibility that it might already be too late.

The hike quickly became intolerable. Hampered by the deep snow, the dense forest, and only a trickle of footprints, the men could not make much progress. At times the trail was so sheer that they slid down hillsides. Other times they had to grab on nearly tree branches to enable them to climb up steep embankments. Three or four times, they crossed Poplar Lick Creek. The water reached mid-calf, and more than once, someone stumbled in the icy stream.

Tired, wet, and suffering from the extreme cold, the team now worried about their own safety. None of them had calculated being this deep in the forest for so many hours.

Refusing to give up, they plunged further into the almost impenetrable woods. After two hours of continuous battery use, their flashlights flickered. With coal mining in his blood, Jr. Brenneman had brought his old coal miner's carbide hat. And that provided the most reliable light for the remainder of their journey.

Hours after they started, they crested a hill. Looking down, the men stopped. A body lay below. Perched on the side of icy Poplar Lick Creek, an airman rested on his frozen haunches, shoulders raised against the biting wind, arms crossed against his chest, and his legs drawn up for protection.

The Lester Bittinger farm on Fairview Road, Garrett County. Photo by Linda Sittig in 2020.

They had found the body of Major Robert L. Payne.

The rescue team approached, and although covered in light layers of snow, they could tell he was not wearing a winter flight suit. In fact, upon closer inspection, it was only a lightweight flight jacket.

The rescue men stood silent, thinking of the desperation that had driven Payne to attempt survival in the face of impossible odds. They also concluded that when Payne, at last, gave in to exhaustion, his eyes had closed, waiting for the gift of final sleep to take him from the nightmare.

Someone radioed back to base camp that they had discovered Major Payne. It was one o'clock in the morning, and they had traveled about two miles from his parachute through the frigid wilderness to find him.

Headquarters asked if the team wanted to return to base and let the military come in the morning to retrieve the body.

The men looked at each other and shook their heads. They weren't going to allow Major Payne to stay out there alone for another night. "We'll bring him in ourselves," they answered.

Base camp replied that the other rescue team would meet them on the road.

Kenneth Resh, Robert Wilt, Ernest Brenneman Jr., George Rexrode, Tom Durst, Martin Tressler, Gary Finzel, Harland Upole, and Joe Durst had coalesced into more than just a rescue team; they were now patriots in the truest sense of the word. And they would leave no man behind.

Exhaustion abounded, but they built a litter out of tree saplings and used a blanket they had brought to tie Major Payne's body on the frame. While two men broke trail, four more carried Major Payne on a slow hike back through the snowy forest. Their advantage was they knew their exact location and could head straight to Savage River Road.

Plodding through the snow and stopping several times to rest and even build a fire to restore some warmth, the rescue group continued on their tortuous journey. No one spoke.

When they emerged on Savage River Road, they met Tom Bender, Blaine Beachy, Jim Michael, Robert Warnick, Dayton Broadwater, Cecil Broadwater, and Hank Handwerk. The second team then assisted with the removal of Major Payne's body to a military helicopter.

It had taken the original group eight and a half hours to find Bob Payne and bring him out of the timberland. From the bleak night, the men emerged to the dawning of a new day.

Major Payne had no knowledge that he had landed in a remote area between two roads. When he finally stopped on the banks of Poplar Lick, he was exactly two and a half miles from either exit point.

As each man in the rescue team trudged home alone, he did so with the indelible image of Robert L. Payne in his mind.

Gary Finzel would say 50 years later, "It was the worst night of my life."

Sterling Queen's Arctic parka. Photo by Linda Sittig, courtesy of Grantsville Museum.

This photo of Savage River State Forest, near where Buzz One Four crashed, shows the difficulty of the terrain faced by the crew as they navigated the blizzard after the crash. Photo courtesy of photographer Tricia Pitcher at https://thedyrt.com/camping/maryland/savage-river-state-forest

Day Four

January 15, 1964

Ten members of the 28th Ordnance Disposal Team of Fort Meade, Maryland, pose for a summer photo. The Ordnance team was responsible for disarming the two nuclear bombs after the crash of Buzz One Four. Photo courtesy of Grantsville Museum.

Christ Lutheran Church, Grantsville, Maryland, where church women cooked and served meals to hundreds of rescue volunteers. Photo courtesy of Christ Lutheran Church.

Wednesday, January 15, 1964
Daytime temperature, Grantsville, Maryland: 9° F

By Wednesday, hundreds of local and military volunteers were combing Savage River State Forest's air and land. Their goal—to find the final missing airman: Melvin Wooten.

The mood never shifted in Garrett County. Everyone was still consumed with finding the last survivor, but the fact that two airmen had been found dead leaned heavily on the human spirit.

Everyone understood that Major Robert Townley had gone down with the plane. But what had caused Major Payne to land where he did?

He had been seated next to Robert Townley in the Black Hole. With Townley out of his seat, desperately trying to get back in his safety harness, maybe Bob Payne stayed, trying to help Townley until the last possible moment. Then Payne ejected, as the final crewman out of the plane.

Strong northeast winds blew the ejected airmen on a southern course. Major Payne had landed further south than the others, approximately 2 miles northwest of the crash site, most likely because he had been the last to depart.

Wednesday brought about other changes.

The Ordnance Team from Fort Meade, who had examined and guarded the bombs, returned to their home base outside Baltimore, Maryland.

The Civil Air Patrol team from West Virginia, who had also guarded the MK-53 bombs and kept all civilians away, were now on their way back home.

The Maryland State Police, including Dick Graham and his K-9 companion, Prince, had returned to their regular duties.

The ladies of the various area churches ceased their frantic pace of daily cooking for the volunteers.

However, the Lonaconing Forestry Boys Camp stayed on alert, and the National Guard Armory in Cumberland kept their cots and canteens service available. The American Red Cross continued to shuttle meals and coffee to the men, still working the crash site.

But the many volunteer cots set up in various locations now sat empty.

The Old Dye Factory Field, West Salisbury, Pennsylvania, where Melvin Wooten landed after ejecting from the plane. Severely hurt and in deep snow, he began to crawl toward the lights of town, to the right in this photo. Photo taken by Linda Sittig, 2020.

Headquarters of New Germany State Park in the 1960s. This was command central for the military coordinating the rescue attempts. Photo courtesy of New Germany State Park.

Day Six

January 17, 1964

Tech Sergeant Melvin D. Wooten – Tailgunner of Buzz One Four, age 27, from Donley, Texas. Photo courtesy of BuzzOneFour.org.

Friday, January 17, 1964
Daytime temperature, Salisbury, Pennsylvania: 55° F

By late Thursday, over 150 local Garrett County local residents had been looking for Tech Sergeant Melvin Wooten, aided by the military groups still in the area.

Each hour, light aircraft took off from the Cumberland Airport, buzzing through the southwestern skies over Savage River State Forest, a landmass of almost 53,000 acres.

As many as 20 helicopters would rise from the parking lots at New Germany State Park, now converted into helipads, and skim through the air like giant dragonflies, looking, always looking for the telltale neon yellow that would signify another parachute.

A few hours in, someone sighted an ejection seat in the area called Pea Ridge, just a few miles south of Route 40. This section near Green Lantern Road was two miles from where the vertical stabilizer had also landed. While the stabilizer, or tail, had gouged itself upright into the earth, two miles away, the ejection seat lay simply on the ground.

Almost entirely intact, the seat seemed to have been the EWO's, the one occupied by Melvin Wooten.

Hopes soared that Melvin Wooten might be in that area.

Groups of rescuers searching for Melvin Wooten now spread out along Pea Ridge. At sixteen, Gerry Beachy received specific instructions – poke at any large lumps in the snow, no telling what might be under a pile.

By dinnertime on Thursday, no further evidence had emerged, and the Army searchers were picked up by helicopters, while Gerry and the local volunteers walked back home.

Discouraged but refusing to admit defeat, the rescuers would rally again tomorrow.

On Friday morning, the temperature warmed and thus melted the top layer of snow.

The daily briefing at the New Germany Park headquarters concluded on a positive note. There were still hundreds of volunteers actively looking for Tech Sergeant Melvin Wooten. Lt. Col. Dale Sauers, the head of the Air Force search and rescue team from Warner Robins, Georgia, felt optimistic.

He looked out over the New Germany parking lot. Vehicle upon vehicle pulled in, loaded with volunteers determined that this would be the day they would find Melvin Wooten.

Major John Voss of the Air Force Strategic Air Command assembled the men into teams and quickly briefed them. Each team would be responsible for a 100-acre search, the size of approximately 100 football fields.

Lt. Col. Frank A. Laboon, US Army, had gathered his men from Fort Belvoir, Virginia, with instructions for today's ground search. One hundred US Marines from Quantico, Virginia, would work side by side with the army today.

Harland Upole, from New Germany Park, and W.A.C. Irwin, district forester, had met with the chief officers of each military division last night. As a group, they mapped out the shoulder-to-shoulder strategy that would be employed by each rescue team.

As Friday morning's search began, helicopters and light aircraft once again took to the skies concentrating now on Pea Ridge.

Hopes ran high. A man could survive for two weeks with an Air Force emergency kit. The talk centered on the possibility that Wooten had been injured and taken refuge in an abandoned barn.

Approximately nine miles north of the New Germany Park headquarters is the community of Salisbury, Pennsylvania. On Friday, 17-year-old Ronald Holler played hooky from school and walked to his grandmother's house to shovel her walk.

Ronald started east and then walked the old B & O tracks toward the community of Boynton. Looking to his right, he noticed some yellow looking material in the Old Dye Factory Field but ignored it.

When he returned home later in the day, he mentioned the yellow to his father. Both Kenneth and Ronald Holler set out to investigate. They approached the Factory Dye Field on Salisbury's northwest side and spied the end of a life raft jutting out from the snow.

They climbed over the farm fencing and trudged through the field. When they came to the life raft, they also discovered an Air Force emergency kit and a parachute.

Looking around, they found tracks in the snow leading away from the life raft and heading toward the Casselman River. They followed the tracks. When they came close to the river, they saw a body stuck upright in the remaining river ice, facing the town.

Telling Ronald to stay put, Mr. Holler walked back down the railroad tracks until he got to a phone and notified the local fire department. It was 3:30 in the afternoon. Within 15 minutes, a group of Salisbury firefighters arrived on the scene.

The tableau in front of them caused each man's shoulders to slump. Young Melvin Wooten had frozen to death in the river. No one needed a coroner to tell them the young man had most likely died the same night he had crashed in the field.

By the direction of his tracks, they concluded he had crawled to reach the lights of town.

In town, Dean Hillegas, a reporter for radio WFRB, heard the news and arrived on the scene as an Air Force helicopter touched down from Cumberland Airport. Within half an hour, three more military choppers arrived. As the Salisbury firemen helped transport Melvin Wooten's body, one member of the military walked off the yardage from the parachute to the river. Melvin Wooten had dragged his injured body 138 yards through the freezing snow.

All in all, the five-man crew had landed within a 12 mile stretch of each other.

The Wooten retrieval team was somber; everyone had hoped that somehow, someway, Melvin Wooten would be discovered alive. Once more, the Base Commander at Turner had to make a painful visit. He had to inform Carol Wooten of the news of her husband.

The knock at the front door came at supper time. Carol turned off the stove and opened the door to find both the Base Commander and the Chaplain on her doorstep. Her heart thumped in her chest.

Through tears, Carol called her mother and then sat down and hugged her children as if she would never let them go.

The next day the Base Commander's wife came over to give whatever comfort she could provide. Without family in the area, Carol was adrift in a sea of grief.

After the Commander's wife left, Carol sat down. She would not be able to stay on base. Their house would be needed for another family, not a widow, not even a 23-year-old widow, with three small children.

A deep sigh escaped her lips. She would have to return home to South Dakota.

11

In researching this book, the one question that I could not definitely answer is, what happened to the bombs?

There are different theories.

According to all the newspaper reports, Ray Giconi, who owned M & S Quarry, brought over his big flat-bed dump trucks, two payloaders with a long bed and short cab, to help with the bomb removal. And even though the Air Force had assured everyone of no impending danger, Ray had borrowed mattresses from the Boys Camp to line the bottom of his truck, to give the bombs a nesting space and chains to secure the bombs in place.

Bob Warnick from the New Germany Park staff had plowed a makeshift road out from the field (crash site), so the bombs could be loaded on trucks and transported to a road.

Ray and his men used front-end loaders to hoist the two nine megaton bombs onto the two flatbeds and proceed to Westernport Road. A military transport provided by Hazelwood Construction met them on the road and ferried the bombs through the back roads to the main highway and the Cumberland Airport. On Thursday, a C-214 Globemaster cargo plane whisked the bombs away to an undisclosed location.

Some newspaper articles say the bombs were moved Wednesday afternoon; others report it to have occurred during Tuesday night. Photos in the Cumberland Times attest to the bombs departing the Cumberland Airport on Thursday, January 16th.

Then there are memories of a parade.

On Thursday afternoon, a caravan of trucks carrying what looked like two big cylinders covered in black tarps motored down into Lonaconing. With Sheriff Paul Haberlein leading the procession, the folks of Lonaconing lined the streets to see the 'bombs' leave their neighborhood.

But, if you talk to enough of the old-timers, they say it would seem highly unlikely that the United States Air Force would allow civilians to move nuclear bombs, much less parade them through a town. "How come we had to guard them bombs for two whole days and not let any civilian near, and then all of a sudden the Air Force lets a quarryman transport them? Nah, those bombs went out Tuesday night under cover of darkness," one old-timer claimed during a July 2020 interview.

And we have the words of Harland Upole, New Germany State Park Superintendent. When asked when the bombs departed, he replied, "Well, we know they were gone by Friday."

The heavily redacted official USAF report (19 of 77 pages blacked out) has virtually no mention of the bombs except for their weight.

Teams assigned to guarding the bombs took an oath of silence.

So, although no one knows for sure when the bombs left, the important thing is that they departed.

Air Force teams hauled massive debris quantities to the Armory at Frostburg for later disbursement to the Strategic Air Command. They also bulldozed immense rubble into large deep pits at the crash site.

While researching this book, I met with the owner of the land where the crash had occurred. His farm is private property with no trespassing allowed. But through a mutual acquaintance, I spent a morning with Frank, walking the terrain.

I was surprised—no, shocked—that pieces of bomber debris kept emerging from the Earth. Wire here, tire sections there, and every once in a while, the sun is glinting off pieces of airplane metal.

At one point, Frank asked me to sniff the ground. An unusual comment, but I complied. There was the lingering smell of airplane fuel; yes, 56 years after the crash, a distinct odor of kerosene and gasoline still oozing from the soil.

When we finished our walk, Frank pointed to an area where the Air Force had dug the huge pits for buried debris.

I remained silent for a minute and then asked him what else the military might have buried in those pits. He looked out, surveying the land, and just shrugged his shoulders.

An hour later, as we sat on his back deck overlooking his fields, a

C-17 appeared in the sky and made a low pass over the land in front of us. It was almost as if the airplane was revisiting hallowed ground.

80

Epilogue

January 18-24, 1964

On Saturday, January 18th, Major Thomas W. McCormick and Captain Parker 'Mack' Peedin flew home to Georgia.

On Monday, January 20th, Major Robert E. Townley was laid to rest in Crestwood Memorial Cemetery, East Gadsden, Alabama.

On the same day, Major Robert L. Payne was laid to rest in the Andersonville National Cemetery, Andersonville, Georgia.

On Friday, January 24th, Tech Sergeant Melvin D. Wooten was laid to rest in the Memory Gardens of Farmington, Farmington, New Mexico.

For the five families of Buzz One Four, life never entirely returned to normal. The legacy of the human drama rippled through the years, often carrying untold sadness.

Remember Major Payne's 1944 lucky silver dollar? Several months after the crash, Fay Payne received a check from the Air Force for one dollar. It was to reimburse her for Bob's silver dollar value. Of course, the value of the coin was sentimental, not monetary.

Another aspect of the tragedy was survivor's guilt.

Major Thomas McCormick stayed in the Air Force and went to Vietnam. However, he requested to take a non-flying job. For the rest of his life, Thomas McCormick experienced frequent bouts of intractable melancholy that he had not been able to save his entire crew.

At one point, Dorismarie suggested they travel, and they took a six-week trip around the globe. His memories of the crash, however, accompanied him.

Thomas McCormick died in 1997 at the age of 76, and is buried in Riverside National Cemetery in Riverside, California. Dorismarie, passed in 2003 at the age of 79 and was laid to rest next to him.

Captain Parker 'Mack' Peedin remained in the Air Force for an additional ten years before switching careers to become a commercial pilot with Pan American Airlines. He and Dianne divorced in 1967, and both remarried.

Mack Peedin also had bouts of the blues. When he did, it often centered around his memories of the crash. Mack died in 2009 at age 74, was cremated, and left behind a second wife.

Dianne Peedin, his first wife, remarried, and in 1979 her second husband, Lt. Col. Charles Arthur Colton, was killed while flying a small airplane for the North Carolina Department of Forest Services. Dianne Peedin Colton passed away in 2003 at age 67 and is buried in Wilmington National Cemetery, Wilmington, North Carolina.

Gene Townley, the widow of Major Robert Edward Townley, went back to Alabama and remarried. At age 90, she died in 2014 and is buried in the same cemetery as Major Townley in Gadsden, Alabama.

After Tech Sergeant Melvin Wooten's burial, his widow, Carol Wooten, returned to her home state of South Dakota and raised her three young children as a single mother. Sixteen years later, Carol and Melvin's son, Jerry Jay Wooten, died in Colorado in an automobile crash.

Many decades later, Carol remarried and is alive as of this writing.

Fay Payne, the widow of Major Robert Lee Payne, stayed in Albany to raise her children but never remarried. Throughout the years, she kept in contact with Bob's family back in Oklahoma. After she passed in 2013 at age 93, she was buried next to him in the Anderson National Cemetery, Macon County, Georgia.

But then there is also serendipity.

Glenna Green Williford was not home the night Buzz One Four crashed a mile from her parents' house. Thirty-seven years later, she was working at the Pentagon when she took a day off from work. That date? 9/11/2001. She missed potential air tragedy twice.

And it is of interest to note that in the Spring of 1964, Mr. Warnick was out plowing a field on his New Germany farm when he discovered Major McCormick's flight book. He dusted it off, and today that flight book is on display in the Grantsville Museum.

Did the crash of Buzz One Four bring about changes in the military?

According to the official report, the Air Force determined the vertical stabilizer's inflight structural failure to the rear bulkhead #1655 caused the plane to crash. On a side note, were four other words:

weather a contributing factor.

Boeing had been alerted for years that the tail on B-52s proved unstable in turbulent air. There had already been numerous incidents, crashes, and crew deaths of B-52s when the tail, or vertical stabilizer, had broken clear from the plane.

But in the middle of The Cold War, the Chrome Dome Missions ran 24 hours a day, as a matter of national security. Every available B-52 had to be ready to fly. Major Robert Payne, Major Robert Townley, and Tech Sergeant Melvin Wooten were not the first American soldiers to give their lives in the line of duty. Nor would they be the last. But the B-52 did go through a series of structural improvements after 1964.

The tragedy of Buzz One Four also remained with the citizens of Garrett County. When the Air Force politely bowed out on the idea of erecting a memorial, Garrett County decided they would preserve the crew's legacy themselves.

Herbert Alexander of Westernport, Maryland, started the process for a permanent monument commemorating the crew's bravery and the rescuers' diligent efforts.

Grantsville formed a committee, sought funding, and planned a parade.

Six months after the crash, on July 4, 1964, hundreds of people lined Main Street in Grantsville under a warm and balmy sky. A 20-unit parade led by the American Legion Color Guard, high school bands, drum and bugle corps, American Red Cross, Girl Scouts, a National Guard Drill Team, and carloads of dignitaries proceeded in patriotic fashion to the edge of town.

As the crowd grew in numbers and arrived at the location of Route 40 and New Germany Road, they stood in rapt attention as a ceremony highlighting the legacy of Buzz One Four's crew began.

The American Legion's Mountain District unveiled a three-sided granite monument inscribed with a tribute to the Garrett County citizens who assisted in the rescue efforts. On the left side is an homage to the three airmen killed in the crash and the two survivors. On the right side is acknowledging the American Air Force's gallantry in protecting American freedom.

This is the center of the monument that stands along Route 40, just east of Grantsville, Maryland. Photo by Linda Sittig.

The ceremony followed with family members sitting across from the speakers' platform where Air Force officials and local dignitaries spoke. Base Commander Brigadier General Woodrow P. Swancutt flew from Turner Air Base to address the crowd. As he finished, the air reverberated with the fly-over of a B-52 Bomber in honor of the Buzz One Four crew.

Most celebrated, however, was Major McCormick and Captain Peedin, who both attended the ceremony. They gave heartfelt thanks to Garrett County citizens for their part in Buzz One Four's rescue attempts and their condolences to the families of the three crewmen who did not survive.

Twelve weeks later, 200 people gathered in West Salisbury, PA, where Melvin Wooten lost his life. Captain Peedin spoke with admiration for Tech Sergeant Wooten. At the memorial marker's unveiling, Mrs. Dianne Peedin accepted a folded American flag to give to Mrs. Carol Wooten, who could not attend because she still had small children at home.

The ceremony concluded with the playing of "Taps."

Then the years and decades sped by. Grantsville initiated a 40th Anniversary Service on July 1, 2004, and the committee placed a large wreath at the foot of the three-sided memorial on Route 40. Fay Payne, Major Payne's widow, and Teresa Payne Chapman, his daughter, and Thomas Payne Chapman, his grandson, all attended the ceremony. A 21-gun salute sounded, and a folded American flag was presented to Major Robert L. Payne's young grandson in memory of his grandfather.

As the 50th anniversary of the crash neared, the Grantsville Community Museum proposed another memorial celebration. Although none of the original crew were still living, most of their children, grandchildren, and extended family members were alive.

Don Townley, son of Major Robert Townley, came to the service holding his father's dog tags, which a farmer had found lying in his property's soil. Michael McCormick, son of Major Thomas McCormick, also attended, thanking Garrett County's people for their heroic attempts in the rescue attempts for all five men.

Carol Wooten, the widow of Sergeant Melvin Wooten, attended with her daughters, who were too young to participate in previous anniversaries.

The service concluded with bagpipes playing "Amazing Grace."

One heartwarming aspect of the tragedy is that several family members of both the crew and the responders kept in touch throughout the years with a friendship borne from tragic circumstances.

Fay Payne and Hazel Klotz wrote to each other over the decades.

The Townley family became friends with the Alexanders of Westernport. And the Alexanders visited Turner Air Force Base, reconnecting with the McCormick and Peedin families.

This photo was taken when several Garrett County people who had been involved with the rescue attempts traveled to Turner Air Force Base to reconnect with Tom McCormick and Mack Peedin. Photo courtesy of Matt McCormick.

More recently, Gina Townley Swinburn and Bucky Schriver have worked together so the Buzz One Four families can remain in touch.

Front row: Carol Wooten, Gina Swinburn's daughters, Haleigh and Nia. Second row: Jeff Bittinger, Deanna Wooten, Debbie Wooten, Gina Townley Swinburn, David Swinburn. Back row: Gretchen Kincer, Norma Green Rollins, Glenna Green Williford. Photo courtesy of Bucky Schriver.

There are now individual, permanent memorials for each airman who did not survive. A simple white marble cross sits near Poplar Lick, where Major Robert Payne lost his life. It was donated and erected by Irwin Memorials of Frostburg. The original dedication took place on July 2, 1964. Because the spot is located 2.5 miles into the forest, Norman Baker and Jack Downton carried the memorial by horse and sled. Today, an accompanying American flag stands in silent witness of Major Payne's courage and determination.

Photo by Bucky Schriver.

Due to the massive amount of wreckage still in the field, Major Robert Townley's memorial was not dedicated until July 4, 1965. A single white marble cross marks where the plane crashed. Townley's marker was donated by the Tri-state Memorial Company of Cresaptown, Maryland, and erected by Herb Alexander and Dick Fazenbaker of Westernport.

July 4, 1965. Front: Gina Townley, Lisa Townley, Reed Townley. Back: George Townley, Margaret Townley, Gene Townley, Weesie Townley. Photo courtesy of Gina Swinburn.

Over the years, wandering cows would rub up against the marker, and so today, it sits inside an enclosure, atop a fieldstone base. Embedded in the stone floor is the top of a replica of a B-52.

Photo by Linda Sittig.

On Sunday, September 27, 1964, the Salisbury Volunteer Fire Department erected a red sandstone memorial to Sergeant Melvin Wooten adjacent to the field where he died.

Resting on a granite base, Johnson Memorials of Meyersdale donated the monument. An American flag flies nearby in salute to Melvin's bravery. Photo by Linda Sittig.

Eagle Scout Aaron Cuppett of Grantsville, Maryland, designed the most recent memorial. Impressed and emotionally moved by the exhibit in the Grantsville Museum, Aaron decided to involve his Boy Scout troop and erect a monument to the fallen crew on public property. The dedication took place on May 25, 2019.

Situated on Westernport Road, just south of Swamp Road, the memorial sits in a tranquil spot of nature as a witness to the men of Buzz One Four.

The trio of Bucky Schriver, Mike Beal, and Eric Alexander continues to volunteer as the memorials' guardians and keep American flags flying next to each monument to alert travelers of these sacred spots.

This is the monument designed by Aaron Cuppett as his Eagle Scout project to honor the crew of Buzz One Four. Photo by Linda Sittig.

Additional Photos

Front row: Kayden Nicol, Helen Nicol, Back Row: Bucky Schriver, Steve Nicol, author Linda Sittig, John Ravenscroft, Steve Timney, Harold Nicol — the author's first interview of people directly involved with the events of the crash. Photo by Jim Sittig.

Bucky Schriver, Linda Sittig, and Frank Sgaggero — current owner of the crash site private property. Photo by Jim Sittig.

Bob Foote, Snowplow operator during the blizzard on January 13, 1964. Photo taken in 2020 by Linda Sittig.

Owner of the crash site farm now, Frank Sgaggero holding a tire from Buzz One Four in 2020. Photo by Linda Sittig.

Norma Green Rollins and Glenna Green Williford at the Green Farmhouse where their parents were the first to hear the crash. Photo by Linda Sittig.

*Jesse and Frances Green who alerted the Maryland State Police about the crash.
Photo courtesy of their daughters Glenna Green Williford and Norma Green Rollins.*

Carbide lamp used in the rescue attempt of Major Robert L. Payne. Photo courtesy of Grantsville Museum.

Photo courtesy of Grantsville Museum.

The crash site July 2020. Photo by Linda Sittig.

The family members of the crew of Buzz One Four, July 12, 2014, Grantsville, MD: Back row: Matt McCormick, Michael McCormick, Tom McCormick. Center row: Mike Davis, Rob Townley, Gina Townley Swinburn, David Swinburn, Bill Chapman, Teresa Payne Chapman, Jeanne McCormick, Benjamin McCormick, Patricia McCormick. Front row: Don Townley, Sharon Townley, Gretchen Hoffbert Kincer, Haleigh Swinburn, Nia Swinburn, Deborah Wooten Gibson, Carol Wooten, Deanna Wooten-Young. Photo courtesy of Gerry Beachy.

PAYNE • TOWNLEY • McCORMICK
484TH BOMBARDMENT WING
WOOTEN
PEEDIN
JANUARY 13, 1964
BUZZ ONE FOUR

Author's Notes

Linda Harris Sittig

In this book, the events and facts were all thoroughly researched. However, I did insert plausible dialog between many of the characters to carry the narrative.

And people still ask about the bombs.

We know from the Air Force report, that together the bombs weighed 17,000 pounds or 8.5 tons. This weight would have strained any quarry's flatbed trucks with typical front-end loaders but still doable.

The explosives were two 9-megaton hydrogen bombs, Mk-53s. Each bomb had the capability of an explosion the equivalent of 9 million tons of TNT. By contrast, the atomic bomb dropped on Hiroshima, Japan, during World War II held 15 kilotons but only had the equivalent explosives of 15,000 tons of TNT. The immediate destruction to Hiroshima occurred within one mile of the explosion. The detonation instantly killed people out in the open. The ensuing firestorm had a destruction path of a five-mile radius, and approximately 140,000 residents died as a result of the bomb.

But a hydrogen bomb has the potential of 1,000 times more destructive power than an atomic bomb of the same size because the hydrogen bomb can cause a more extensive explosion, shock wave, blast, heat, and radiation. According to nuclear scientists, a hydrogen bomb would most likely have an immediate destructive radius of five to ten miles. All buildings within nine miles would collapse, and people within 20 miles would receive fatal burns if they were outside.

And Buzz One Four carried two of those bombs whose radiation cloud would have affected West Virginia, Maryland, Virginia, and Pennsylvania.

These hydrogen bombs were the core of SAC's Chrome Dome Missions. If the Soviet Union deployed a nuclear weapon against the United States, Air Force B-52s would be able within 30 minutes to strike back with detonating explosives against a Russian target that could wipe out all nearby life.

Almost immediately on the Monday following the crash, the Pentagon issued a joint statement with the Eighth Air Force that the bombs were inactive all along and not an immediate danger. They attempted to reassure civilians that B-52s carrying nuclear devices have a complex set of safety mechanisms to prevent an accidental nuclear detonation. However, they also stipulated that no civilian should go anywhere near the wreckage debris.

For the people whose homes were close to the crash site, that statement didn't calm their fears. Did radiation leak into the soil? With a potential capacity of 37,000 gallons of jet fuel sinking into the Earth, was the underground water table affected?

Even today, fear lingers.

And this was the 5th such accident in the United States of a B-52 bomber carrying nuclear weapons, a Fifth American Broken Arrow.

Where and when were the other Broken Arrows that occurred in the United States?

A total of 32 documented Broken Arrows have occurred since 1950. The first one in the U.S. occurred on February 5, 1958, over Tybee Island, Georgia when a B -47 bomber carrying a single Mark 15 nuclear bomb collided with an F-86 fighter jet.

The crew of the B-47 requested permission to jettison the bomb. The bomb landed in the sea at Wassaw Sound, and there were no casualties. After many searches, the bomb has never been located.

One can only assume it still lies buried in the waters off Tybee Island today.

The next Broken Arrow to occur in America was on March 11, 1958, when a B -47 took off from Hunter Air Force Base in Savannah, Georgia, with a Mark 6 nuclear bomb on board.

Shortly after takeoff, the fault light indicated that a bomb harness locking pin had not engaged. The Navigator went below to investigate and mistakenly grabbed the emergency release pin.

That action forced the Mark 6 Bomb to drop into the bomb bay, and the weight then drove the bomb doors open. The bomb dropped out of the plane over Mars Bluff, South Carolina.

Below on the ground, three young girls were playing. The bomb landed within 200 yards of them and the explosives detonated. Although the girls survived, six civilians were seriously injured, and seven nearby buildings were significantly damaged.

Then came March 14, 1961. A B-52 Stratofortress inadvertently ran out of fuel in flight and was unable to refuel mid-air. With the fuel nearly depleted, the crew ejected near Yuba City, California. The crewless plane flew an additional 15 miles and crashed west of Yuba City.

The four nuclear weapons onboard did not detonate.

Broken Arrow number four occurred on January 23, 1961, as a B-52 carrying two 3-4 Megaton Mark 39 nuclear bombs broke apart in mid-air near Goldsboro, North Carolina.

The pilot ordered the eight-man crew to eject at 9,000 feet. Five men survived, and three died during the ejection and subsequent crash.

One of the bombs plunged at 700 miles per hour into a muddy field, and parts are still buried 180 feet below the earth's surface.

Buzz One Four would become the Fifth Broken Arrow. Eventually, other Broken Arrows occurred over the Mediterranean, Greenland, and British Columbia. The official reports show a total of 32 Broken Arrows.

How and when did the accidents stop?

The Chrome Dome missions ended in 1968, and so did the Broken Arrows.

Today, in the Grantsville Museum, a superb exhibit depicts the story of Buzz One Four's crash, the rescue attempts, and the enduring legacy. Curated by Gerry Beachy and his wife, Sue, it stands in testimony that people still care. Yes, the same Gerry Beachy, who, as a 16-year-old, spent hours pushing through waist-high snow on Pea Ridge with US Army volunteers hoping to find Melvin Wooten, the last airman.

As I finish writing this book, I am still humbled by the efforts of hundreds of people who came together in Garrett and Allegany Counties to try and save the lives of five men they had never met. After all the research, images of compassion, bravery, and human decency resound in my mind.

For my own needed closure, I visited the memorials in the summer of 2020. With my head bowed in prayer in front of the stones, I whispered, "You are not forgotten."

Respectfully Written,
Linda Harris Sittig
Purcellville, Virginia

Acknowledgements

I pored over every magazine and newspaper article written on the crash and found multiple discrepancies. I then realized I had to dive deeper into the research and connect with people who had been involved with the tragedy. I completed a total of 34 interviews and consulted with Air Force personnel for the veracity of facts.

I am forever grateful to the following people:

To my Beta Readers: Thomas A. Dunn III (a former Captain United States Air Force), Laura Savino (a former United Airlines Pilot), Bucky Schriver (local Maryland historian), and Gina Swinburn (niece of Major Robert E. Townley). All of you read and re-read through my drafts and helped me deliver the message as clearly as possible.

John Josselyn created the excellent website BUZZONEFOUR.ORG in honor of the crew. Matt McCormick, Major Thomas McCormick's grandson, made the superb documentary BUZZ ONE FOUR, available on Amazon Prime. Rounding up the visual research was Renee Green, who filmed BUZZ ONE FOUR: RESCUE, RECOVERY & IMPACT, a well-researched documentary about the crash and the people of Garrett County.

A sincere thank you to the following 34 individuals who allowed me to interview them and hear their memories about the crew or the crash. Others shared their experiences about military bases.

Gina Townley Swinburn, Lisa Townley Gilbeaux, Weesie Townley, Joyce Bowman, Roger Williams, Fred and Pat Harris, Matt McCormick, Sterling Queen, Dwight Bittinger, Steve Timney, Harold and Helen Nicol, John Ravenscroft, Rose Schriver, Bucky Schriver, Frank Sgaggero, Glenna Green Williford, Norma Green Rollins, Bob Foote, Mark Alexander, Carol Wooten, Janet Graham, Ray Andrews, Gerry and Sue Beachy, Teresa Payne

Chapman, George Menser, Roger Williams, Tamra Warnick, John Josselyn, Allen Broadwater, Eric Alexander, and Leo Mills.

Another thank you to Erin Thomas of New Germany State Park for pinpointing which of the present-day cabins was the former park headquarters. Thank you to Amy Godwin of Dyrt.com for arranging clearance for me to use their photo of the Savage River State Forest.

A special thanks to George Menser for his expertise as a retired Master Sergeant for the US Air Force who performed maintenance on B-52 bombers and provided me with many technical details. Roger Williams flew B-52 bombers as the EWO (Electronic Warfare Officer) as a First Lt. Captain, US Air Force, in the 1960s. He shared his first-hand knowledge about the Chrome Dome Operations. Fred Harris related his memories of being a Colonel in the US Air Force stationed in Georgia. His wife, Pat Harris, shared memories of what life on an American Air Force Base was like for military wives. Steve Slaughter, former commander of the USAF Jump Team, helped with the parachute calculations.

And as always, a thank you to Liz Eshelman, the President of the Frostburg Museum, who cheerfully assists me in all of my research requests!

Of all the reports and articles about the crash, David Wood's article, Bomber Down, was the most accurate, printed on August 8, 1999, Washington Post Magazine. Lou Drendel's book, B-52 Stratofortress Illustrated was the book I turned to time and again to make sure I knew what a B-52 looked like from the inside out.

I also learned how to set a narrative platform from Jim Defede in his book, The Day the World Came to Town, and Tod Olson with his book, Lost in the Pacific, 1942.

And as always, I am indebted to the wonderful staff at Freedom Forge Press, especially my former publisher Eric Egger and my editor, Val Muller, who believe along with me, that freedom is never truly free.

In closing, a sincere thank you to Bucky Schriver, who started me on the journey. And to my husband Jim Sittig, who once again put his daily activities on hold to drive me around Garrett and Allegany Counties, trying to recreate the story while we stood in the footprints of history.

The Wives of Buzz One Four Airmen

Mrs. Dorismarie McCormick – Major Thomas McCormick's wife
Mrs. Fay Payne – Major Robert Payne's wife
Mrs. Dianne Peedin – Captain Mack Peedin's wife
Mrs. Imogene 'Gene' Townley – Major Robert Townley's wife
Mrs. Carol Wooten – Tech Sergeant Melvin Wooten's wife

- all strong women -

The People Involved in the Story

Cecil B. Arthur
Emerson Alexander
Eric Alexander
Herbert Alexander
Mark Alexander
Ray Andrews
Normand Baker
Blaine Beachy
Gerry Beachy and Sue Beachy
Tom Durst
Carl Ellenburg
Gary Finzel
Bob Foote
Ray Giconi
Dick Graham
Jesse and Frances Green
Glenna and Norma Green
Paul Haberlein
Hank Handwerk
Milt Hart
Dean Hillegas
Kenneth Holler
Ronald Holler
W.A.C. Irwin
Ray Jenkins
Hazel Klotz
Frank A. Laboon, Lt. Colonel, USAF
Roy Lambert
John "Babe" Layton
Michael McCormick
Jim Michael
Harold and Helen Nicol
Sterling Queen

Tom Bender
Lester Bittinger
Ernest Brenneman, Jr.
Cecil Broadwater
Dayton Broadwater
Aaron Cuppett
Mike Beal
Jack Downton
Joe Durst
Bill Ramsey
John and Robert Ravenscroft
Kenneth Resh
George Rexrode
Dale Sauers, Lt. Colonel, USAF
Bucky Schriver
Rose Schriver
Frank Sgaggero
Joseph Stakem
Steve Timney
Don Townley
Gina Townley Swinburn
Lis Townley Gilbeaux
Martin Tressler
Harland Upole
John Voss, Major
Robert, Daniel, and Kathleen Warnick
Tamra Warnick and Bob Warnick
Asa Wilhelm
Robert Wilt
James Brenneman Mills
Leo Mills
Teresa Payne

Woodrow P. Swancutt, Base Commander and Brigadier General, USAF

About the author

Born in Greenwich Village, New York City, and raised in Northern New Jersey, Linda was lured into reading by *Lad, a Dog* and *Nancy Drew, Girl Detective*. Later her attraction to history and a bit of wanderlust led her to study in Switzerland, before returning stateside to earn a B.A. in History and a M.Ed. in Reading. Linda eventually chose to live in Loudoun County, Virginia, where the beauty of the Blue Ridge Mountains inspired her to write. Today, Linda and her husband live in North Carolina, still near the Blue Ridge.

Combining her passion for history, stories, and the need for literacy, she began publishing commentaries on how parents could encourage the love of reading with their children. That led to a twenty-year weekly newspaper column, "KinderBooks" (*Loudoun Times-Mirror*); a non-fiction text, *New Kid in School* (Teachers College Press); and writing for a nationally syndicated educational newsletter, *The Connection* (PSK Associates).

Linda was twice recognized by the Virginia Press Association with Certificates of Merit for her journalism. Her articles have appeared in *The Washington Post*, *The Reston Connection*, and *Chicken Soup for the Soul*, in addition to numerous professional journals and short story anthologies. Passionate about lesser known women in history who led extraordinary lives, Linda blogs monthly at www.strongwomeninhistory.com, and has followers in over 64 countries.

From 1982 – 1994 Linda received three separate distinguished educator awards from metropolitan, state, and international organizations. She recently retiring from teaching at Shenandoah University in Winchester, VA, where she worked with educators on how to immerse literature into children's lives.

Linda is also the author of *Cut From Strong Cloth*, *Last Curtain Call*, *Counting Crows* and *Opening Closed Doors: The Story of Josie Murray*.

Email: Linda@LindaSittig.com
Website: www.LindaSittig.com
Blog: www.strongwomeninhistory.com

"Every woman deserves to have her story told."

www.ingramcontent.com/pod-product-compliance
Lightning Source LLC
Chambersburg PA
CBHW070909160726
48004CB00003B/1297